LOS ANGELES 200

A Bicentennial Celebration

Text by
ART SEIDENBAUM

Photographs by
JOHN MALMIN

Foreword by
WILL DURANT

LOS ANGELES 200

A Bicentennial Celebration

Harry N. Abrams, Inc.,
Publishers, New York

Will Durant

A LOVE AFFAIR WITH THE QUEEN OF THE ANGELS

How could I help but fall in love with a city named after Nuestra Senora la Reina de Los Angeles (Our Lady the Queen of the Angels)? In my childhood I had been a happy pupil in a happy circle dancing around a Sister of Charity, all singing songs of praise to the Mother of God. What better dedication could a city have than to recall the modest maiden who had fearfully undertaken to bear divinity?

I don't suppose that such tender sentiments moved me when in 1943 I led my little family from Great Neck, Long Island, on a drive across the continent amid a congestion of martial traffic. Our New York neighbors sent us off with a merry song, "California, here we come." Our friend of Grand Rapids days, Jim Fifield, who had become minister of the First Congregational Church in Los Angeles, helped us find a home in the Hollywood Hills—one of the many houses abandoned in the fear that the Japanese would repeat in Los Angeles their reckless triumph at Pearl Harbor. The building had been neglected, with broken windows welcoming the rain; the twenty-year-old structure was surrounded by weeds taller than men. We bought the ruin, repaired it, have lived in it contentedly now for thirty-seven years, and pray for the privilege of dying there whenever the Reaper finds us fit for remolding.

Monogamous in cities as well as in mates, I needed little urging to write a word of welcome to this story of the spreading metropolis that, with whatever faults of air or men, is for me still a gift of the gods. It is not the city's fault that its sky has been tarnished by the breath of its cars and industries; we may hope that this blight will be mitigated by the end of the reign of oil. Then we shall see King Sol march triumphantly, nearly every day, from the Rockies to the sea, and we shall complain bitterly of our blistered skin and blinded eyes.

Or we may worry about the exhaustion of oil wells and forests and the compulsion to return to coal to fire our engines and warm our homes. But new oil is found in unexpected places, foresters know how to replace the trees they cut down, and I look back without terror to the years when I had to shovel coal into the furnace and stove. More difficult are the problems of war, which I leave to the nation rather than to the cities, and the puzzle of ethnic diversity. I speak with unusual hesitation here since I, though native born, am of French-Canadian heritage and cannot share with intimacy the fear of the old stocks that they will soon be a minority in population and then in political and military power. Can our new stocks be infused with the national unity, resolution, and pride that came to our Anglo-Saxon leaders from their sense of inheriting the blood of the founding fathers and can they be infused with some of the bold intelligence that created the American Republic and wrote its stirring documents? Can we induce our schools and industries, our minds and hearts, to welcome our new Americans into the mainstream of national life?

I believe that this book, though with no such specific aim, will show us how a small pueblo, nestling below the San Bernardino Mountains against northern winds, took into itself almost every year newcomers asking permission to work a bit of land on which to earn a shelter for their brood and will also show us how these lusty increments, however diverse, in time helped to form a united and vigorous community. So, I believe, our various ethnic groups, while justifiably clinging to their roots and cherished ways, will be drawn into a proud and happy unity, not only by our schools and colleges and industries but by the very ardor and sweep of American life. Let us hope and labor to that end.

Art Seidenbaum
INTRODUCTION

The rest of the world has always wondered what to make of Los Angeles, a sprawling city of 465 square miles in a sprawling county of the same name covering 4,000 square miles of mountain, coastline, desert, and dirt. This mammoth and incredibly diffuse stretch of imagination spreads almost beyond definition. Tourists and residents alike have emphasized Los Angeles as a paradox, since they lack a cohesive way to approach something so big, so peculiar, so contradictory: sunshine versus natural disasters; gaudy show business as opposed to a walled-in population seeking privacy; strange cults opposite a history of fierce independence; a collection of paradoxes, with a community that is sometimes in search of a centralized downtown, but more often in celebration of its scattered diversity.

Los Angeles frequently has not known what to make of itself, starting with those first forty-four pioneers who trekked north from Mexico to settle a trading outpost for Spain. The rich and productive era of the ranchos was followed by the decline of the missions and finally independence from Mexico. Los Angeles was named capital of California for a brief period under Mexican rule, but the city fathers were not concerned enough to establish a proper political base for local government.

That's not surprising. This is a city without much pomp or pretension, and being a capital would have imposed certain formalities on it. Social scientists like to stress the fashions or fads begun in Southern California and then exported to the rest of the country. Styles do indeed originate in Los Angeles, but the city doesn't much care about being the capital of new notions any more than it once cared about being the capital of California. Local pride is more personal than provincial. Residents rarely brag about being in Los Angeles.

The American flag has flown over the city only since the middle of the nineteenth century, billowing above land booms, oil booms, movie booms, and, more literally, the sonic booms of aerospace. Speculation—financial, technological, sociological—has punctuated the intervening years, the speculation of a people continually wondering what to make of a confounding culture.

Perhaps this sense of what is still undone, this open-ended sense of space and time and opportunity, is the conspicuous reason for an enduring optimism. New groups of foreigners, whether from Asia or Europe or the rest of the United States, are being assimilated or accommodated as continuing chapters in this unfinished urban story.

And now the story reaches a bicentennial punctuation mark: 200 years from tiny pueblo to powerful city. This book records those 200 years—now and then, then and now—marking annual chapters of the story in text and illustrating each of them with contemporary pictures. The photography is the city as it stands at the beginning of the 1980s. The narrative describes how the city became this way. Each photograph is connected to an historical event, perhaps being the first attempt to illuminate the visual present in terms of a year-by-year record of the past.

Photographer John Malmin and I have been making these connections—pictures of now linked to text from then, megalopolitan present tied to pastoral beginnings—for three years. For John this is the culminating *Los Angeles Times* task, winding up four decades of photographic excellence with the assignment from editor Bill Thomas to do this book. For me this is a sort of ultimate treat, trying to make something informative as well as something beautiful of a city I came to live in twenty-one years ago and quickly came to love.

We had extraordinary help along the way, from the Huntington Library, UCLA Special Collections, the Plaza Church, First Century Families, county and city government, as well as from hundreds of other organizations and individuals.

Our self-imposed boundaries were the borders of Los Angeles County for photography, although early Los Angeles embraced just about all the land up from San Diego and down from Santa Barbara. We made a few exceptions by including important aspects of Orange and Ventura counties, and we went up the coast for sea otters because they are only slowly reappearing around Los Angeles.

One major surprise: in the midst of urbanization was the persistence of rural life—the sheep, horses, cattle, and grain still thriving within Los Angeles's borders. Pastoral lands are still to be found in Antelope Valley and western San Fernando Valley.

Weather worked both for and against us. During the course of John's camera rounds, there were a few earthquakes and landslides, several fires, and dozens of smog attacks. Some of those calamities are captured in the illustrations. But since earthquakes are not photogenic, we wound up simulating the great shakes. Smog looks worse in reality than through the lens, perhaps because the eye of a camera is not so easily irritated as that of a human.

Some pictures required months of planning, such as the portrait of the county Board of Supervisors because these administrators rarely stand still for group ceremony. Other pictures, such as the wonder of snow in Southern California, required only the lucky moment of being where the unexpected happens.

We spent more time at educational institutions than at motion picture studios, more weeks scouting residential neighborhoods than amusement parks, realizing that homegrown attractions count for everyday flavor more importantly than tourist attractions. Los Angeles is a city of "Let be," of citizens who define themselves by what they do in search of the good life rather than by what job they do in search of a comfortable living. The hurrahs of show business and the marvels of aerospace business are fanfares of local life; they are not the profound conditions of a society willing to allow each person a private pursuit.

We were constantly reminded of the cultures that make up this extraordinarily cosmopolitan community: native Americans, Asians, Europeans, Hispanics, Africans—black, white, beige, copper people from every cranny of every continent. The history of Los Angeles has its bloody chapters of ethnic violence, but that same history tends to embrace—and at last recognize—the considerable contributions from every group.

A 200th birthday party is the perfect occasion for congratulating the more than seven million people residing in the county, including the three million within the city itself. We like to think of this book as a family album, bound in affection, glued together with truth. What these settlers have made of Los Angeles—in the face of ravaging fires, fierce earthquakes, water shortages, shaky geology, great distances, and ever-changing demography—is a remarkably habitable city with a brilliant rainbow range of individuals. We are looking here at a human story of amalgamation from contradiction, affirmation from paradox.

Franciscan
missionary

1791
Only a decade
after first
settlement
grain harvest
is impressive

1792
Pueblo
becomes haven
for retired
Spanish
soldiers

1793
Small force of
soldiers from
Santa Barbara
assigned to the
pueblo

1794
Neophytes
attached to
San Gabriel
Mission
number 1,000

1795
Spanish
authorities
promote animal
husbandry at
pueblo

1796
After biggest
harvest ever,
pueblo begins
to ship grain to
Santa Barbara

1797
Father Fermin
Lasuen founds
San Fernando
Mission

1798
First jail built
by Alcalde Soto

1799
Still only 30
adobe buildings
make up the
little pueblo

1800
Livestock
increasing at
a rate greater
than humans

California
ranchero

Rancho land
grant

1831
Traders arrive
from Santa Fe;
many more will
follow in the
decade ahead

1832
Governor Don
Victoria forced
to flee to
Mexico
by local
uprising

1833
Mexico orders
secularization
of the missions

1834
Pio Pico, one
of the last
Mexican
governors,
is married
in the pueblo

1835
Mexico decrees
that Los
Angeles be the
future capital of
California

1836
First hanging by
a vigilante mob

1837
Juan Bandini
captures Los
Angeles, only
to leave a few
days later

1838
Los Angeles
government
closes year
with surplus of
only $3

1839
Grants of
ranchos
continue,
spurred by the
secularization
of missions

1840
Abel Stearns, a
prominent
American,
arraigned on
charges of
smuggling

Los Angeles in
1870s

The Plaza

1871
Lynch mob
murders 19
Chinese in
pogrom

1872
First public
library opens,
funded by
subscription

1873
Orange Grove
Association
begins to
develop what
will become
Pasadena

1874
Construction of
Point Fermin
lighthouse

1875
Tiburcio
Vasquez,
notorious
bandit, is
hanged

1876
Southern
Pacific Railroad
reaches Los
Angeles

1877
New reservoir
built atop
Bunker Hill

1878
2,720 couples
married in Los
Angeles

1879
Old wharf
torn down
at Santa
Monica

1880
University of
California
founded

Sixth and
Spring streets

Venice

1911
California
adopts its state
flag

1912
Los Angeles
Athletic Club
opens

1913
Aqueduct
opens, bringing
water from
Owens Valley

1914
Jitney buses
appear but
lose out to
trolleys

1915
San Fernando
Valley is
annexed to the
city

1916
Film industry
booms

1917
Construction
begins on
Hollyhock
House designed
by Frank
Lloyd Wright

1918
Downtown
congestion
eased by
opening of
Second Street
tunnel

1919
Los Angeles
Philharmonic
formed

1920
Los Angeles
becomes the
seventh most
populous city
in the country

Opening of
Disneyland,
1955

1951
Baldwin Hill
reservoir
constructed
to service
growing
population

1952
City's growing
pains result in
racial hostility
and bombings
of black homes

1953
USC Trojans
at last win
in Rose Bowl,
demolishing
myth of Big 10
superiority

1954
To reduce
smog, county
bans backyard
incinerating

1955
Walt Disney
opens a magic
kingdom called
Disneyland

1956
After height
limitation
on buildings
is dropped,
skyscrapers
start to rise

1957
The Otis Art
Institute's new
building opens,
commemorating
H. G. Otis

1958
Bunker Hill
redevelopment
Project is
authorized for
downtown area

1959
Citizens group
saves Watts
Towers, an
outstanding
work of
folk art

1960
The backyard
swimming pool
becomes
symbol of local
life-style

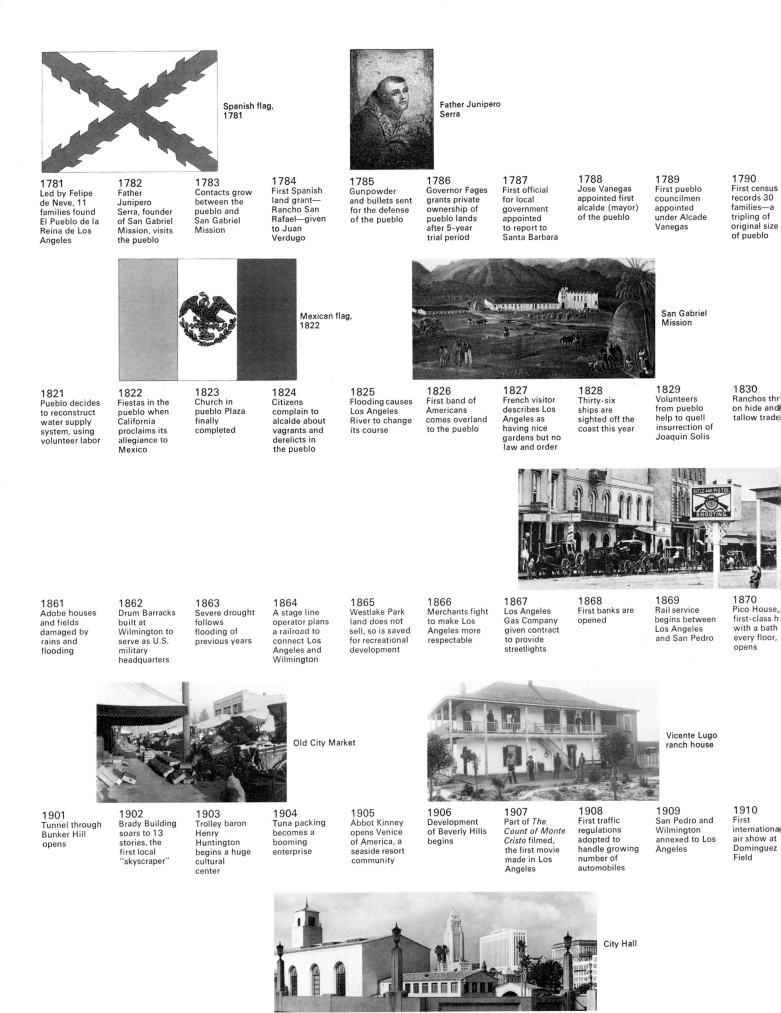

Spanish flag, 1781

Father Junipero Serra

1781
Led by Felipe de Neve, 11 families found El Pueblo de la Reina de Los Angeles

1782
Father Junipero Serra, founder of San Gabriel Mission, visits the pueblo

1783
Contacts grow between the pueblo and San Gabriel Mission

1784
First Spanish land grant—Rancho San Rafael—given to Juan Verdugo

1785
Gunpowder and bullets sent for the defense of the pueblo

1786
Governor Fages grants private ownership of pueblo lands after 5-year trial period

1787
First official for local government appointed to report to Santa Barbara

1788
Jose Vanegas appointed first alcalde (mayor) of the pueblo

1789
First pueblo councilmen appointed under Alcade Vanegas

1790
First census records 30 families—a tripling of original size of pueblo

Mexican flag, 1822

San Gabriel Mission

1821
Pueblo decides to reconstruct water supply system, using volunteer labor

1822
Fiestas in the pueblo when California proclaims its allegiance to Mexico

1823
Church in pueblo Plaza finally completed

1824
Citizens complain to alcalde about vagrants and derelicts in the pueblo

1825
Flooding causes Los Angeles River to change its course

1826
First band of Americans comes overland to the pueblo

1827
French visitor describes Los Angeles as having nice gardens but no law and order

1828
Thirty-six ships are sighted off the coast this year

1829
Volunteers from pueblo help to quell insurrection of Joaquin Solis

1830
Ranchos thr on hide and tallow trade

1861
Adobe houses and fields damaged by rains and flooding

1862
Drum Barracks built at Wilmington to serve as U.S. military headquarters

1863
Severe drought follows flooding of previous years

1864
A stage line operator plans a railroad to connect Los Angeles and Wilmington

1865
Westlake Park land does not sell, so is saved for recreational development

1866
Merchants fight to make Los Angeles more respectable

1867
Los Angeles Gas Company given contract to provide streetlights

1868
First banks are opened

1869
Rail service begins between Los Angeles and San Pedro

1870
Pico House, first-class h with a bath every floor, opens

Old City Market

Vicente Lugo ranch house

1901
Tunnel through Bunker Hill opens

1902
Brady Building soars to 13 stories, the first local "skyscraper"

1903
Trolley baron Henry Huntington begins a huge cultural center

1904
Tuna packing becomes a booming enterprise

1905
Abbot Kinney opens Venice of America, a seaside resort community

1906
Development of Beverly Hills begins

1907
Part of *The Count of Monte Cristo* filmed, the first movie made in Los Angeles

1908
First traffic regulations adopted to handle growing number of automobiles

1909
San Pedro and Wilmington annexed to Los Angeles

1910
First internationa air show at Dominguez Field

City Hall

1941
World War II causes aircraft boom, bringing $550 million to local companies

1942
Doolittle's raid on Tokyo is turning point after defeats in the Pacific

1943
Wartime racial tensions erupt in "Zoot Suit" riots between sailors and Hispanics

1944
First release of Japanese-Americans from internment camps during the war

1945
Peace brings many changes, prosperity, new residents, new products

1946
Parking meters introduced for needed revenue in spite of opposition

1947
Public enemy called smog is target of new laws and control board

1948
Television invades Los Angeles, changes entertainment business

1949
Postwar recreation is centered more on beach activities

1950
Population Los Angele zooms to 2 million, wit urban spra growing ap

YEAR BY YEAR

Calle de los Negros

n
ction
s
nts
pain and

1812
Los Angeles suffered in what is known as the "Year of the Earthquakes"

1813
Missions resist secularization ordered by Spanish government

1814
Missionaries sell brandy to build a church in the Plaza, but spirits soon run out

1815
Los Angeles drenched by torrential rains lasting for 10 days

1816
Mission padres fear growing holdings and power of rancho owners

1817
First school opens in the pueblo but its only teacher soon leaves

1818
Work resumes on Plaza church, funded this time by sale of donated cattle

1819
Piracy and poaching by foreign sailors increase along the coast

1820
New squabbles over grazing rights—this time padres point accusing finger

The pueblo from Fort Hill

Rancho La Brea

armers
t El
first
nity
d by
ans

1852
Legal battles waged over land grants made prior to the annexation

1853
Methodist and Presbyterian preachers establish churches

1854
County funds authorized for building a wagon road to Fort Tejon

1855
Another try at public education gets lukewarm public support

1856
French sailor opens café and beer garden, where concerts are held for the public

1857
City authorizes building of a waterworks system

1858
Butterfield Stage Line brings overland mail service

1859
First city market opens

1860
Attempt made to construct sidewalks out of tar from the La Brea pits

Belmont

Los Angeles oil wells

Cahuenga Avenue and Hollywood Boulevard

n citrus
egins

1892
First oil well, dug on residential lot

1893
Completion of Bradbury Building, designed by George Wyman

1894
Economic depression hits Los Angeles

1895
Electric trolley links downtown with Westlake Park

1896
San Pedro named as site for harbor, ending years of debate

1897
Los Angeles Symphony established, the first orchestra west of the Rockies

1898
G. J. Griffith donates over 3,000 acres to the city for a park

1899
The horseless carriage begins to be seen on city streets

1900
Chamber of Commerce makes national blitz to promote Los Angeles

The unemployed at Plaza Church

Hyperion Avenue

—Ocean
nnual
w, 1923

Bridge
idena
ed to
future
eaps

1932
Tenth modern Olympic Games held in Los Angeles before record crowds

1933
Earthquake splits streets and shatters buildings, killing 120

1934
Santa Anita Racetrack built, 1 year after track betting was legalized

1935
Pan-Pacific Auditorium opens, an optimistic grand gesture in hard times

1936
Los Angeles police turn away 1,000 migrants a day who are job hunting

1937
Los Angeles develops plans for public transportation system

1938
Scandal at City Hall brings in reform mayor at city's nadir

1939
Union Station opens 2 years after Super Chief begins fast service to Chicago

1940
Freeway to Pasadena opens new era in auto travel

Aftermath of earthquake

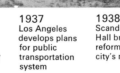

Panorama, looking east from Wilshire Boulevard

nic
and
uake
egion

1972
Broadway Plaza reverses trend and brings shopping center downtown

1973
Arab oil embargo causes energy crisis in city dependent on the automobile

1974
Oil tycoon J. Paul Getty gives city an art museum in a Roman villa

1975
Art Center College of Design campus begun in hills above Pasadena

1976
Diamond Lanes on freeways introduced to modify car usage—with no success

1977
Rodeo Drive in Beverly Hills becomes the ultimate international bazaar

1978
Malibu fire burns path from Santa Monica Mountains to Malibu Beach

1979
Severe winter of snow and rain startles inhabitants of California

1980
Los Angeles looks ahead— another century, more Olympics, a sunny future

Mission Indians

1801 Heavy rains cause the Porciuncula River to flood

1802 Rancho El Conejo, between the pueblo and Santa Barbara, is settled

1803 American and Russian hunters active along coastal area

1804 Malibu begins as a remote rancho founded by Jose Bartolome Tapia

1805 First American visits Los Angeles—Captain William Shaler

1806 Orchards planted at San Gabriel Mission

1807 Trading by foreign ships continues, in defiance of Spanish law

1808 Landings by British seamen revealed when Indian brings Union Jack to San Fernando

1809 California hit by drought, especially severe around Los Angeles

1810 Soldiers again protest having to capture runaway neophytes

1811 Mexic insurre disrup shipm from S Mexic

Pio Pico

United States flag, 1848

1841 B. D. Wilson arrives in the pueblo that in a decade will elect him mayor

1842 Gold is discovered in Placerita Canyon above San Fernando Mission

1843 Mexican authority and control diminish daily

1844 Two squadrons of cavalry formed for the defense of the pueblo

1845 Battle of Cahuenga Pass ends in confusion

1846 Formal declaration of the Mexican-American War

1847 Americans take the pueblo and begin building Fort Moore

1848 Los Angeles becomes part of the United States

1849 First survey made of the new American town

1850 Los Angeles declared a self-governing city

1851 Texas settle Monte comm found Ameri

Main Street

Hotel fire

1881 Los Angeles celebrates its centennial, with speeches in English and Spanish

1882 Introduction of the telephone to Los Angeles

1883 Los Angeles Board of Trade established

1884 Charles Lummis, later the city librarian, walks to town from Cincinnati

1885 Socialist politician plans road named after him—Wilshire Boulevard

1886 Hordes arrive as rail fares drop in rate war

1887 Real estate boom promotes overnight communities, but not all take root

1888 Collapse of the "Boom of the Eighties"

1889 Rose Tournament sponsors chariot races

1890 City receives land for what will become Hollenbeck Park

1891 Boom fruits

Shooting a movie

Venic Park Revie

1921 Spadina House designed as a movie set; later moved to Beverly Hills

1922 First tract known as Westwood developed

1923 Biltmore Hotel completed amid another real estate boom

1924 Three planes made by Donald Douglas are first to fly around the world

1925 Venice votes to become part of Los Angeles after heated local debate

1926 Evangelist Aimee Semple McPherson disappears in the surf off Ocean Park

1927 Speed limit of 40 mph is imposed

1928 The new City Hall opens

1929 UCLA opens the first buildings of its new campus in Westwood

1930 In spite of the Depression Beverly Hills prospers and brags of record growth

1931 Suicid in Pas is alte preven death

Watts riots

Robert F. Kennedy at Ambassador Hotel

1961 Sam Yorty is elected mayor for first of 3 terms. His gut issue—garbage

1962 Plan announced for mammoth urban complex, called Century City, on old Fox lot

1963 First large bridge built; Vincent Thomas links Terminal Island with San Pedro

1964 Dorothy Chandler Pavilion opens at Los Angeles Music Center

1965 Visual arts given their due when County Art Museum opens

1966 Hippies and exotic cults emerge as social signs of the times

1967 Bunker Hill project moves ahead with grading of 136 downtown acres

1968 Robert Kennedy assassinated at Ambassador Hotel after state primary victory

1969 City and county merge in the administration of the area's beaches

1970 Integration of Los Angeles schools ordered by Superior Court

1971 Econo slump earthq shake

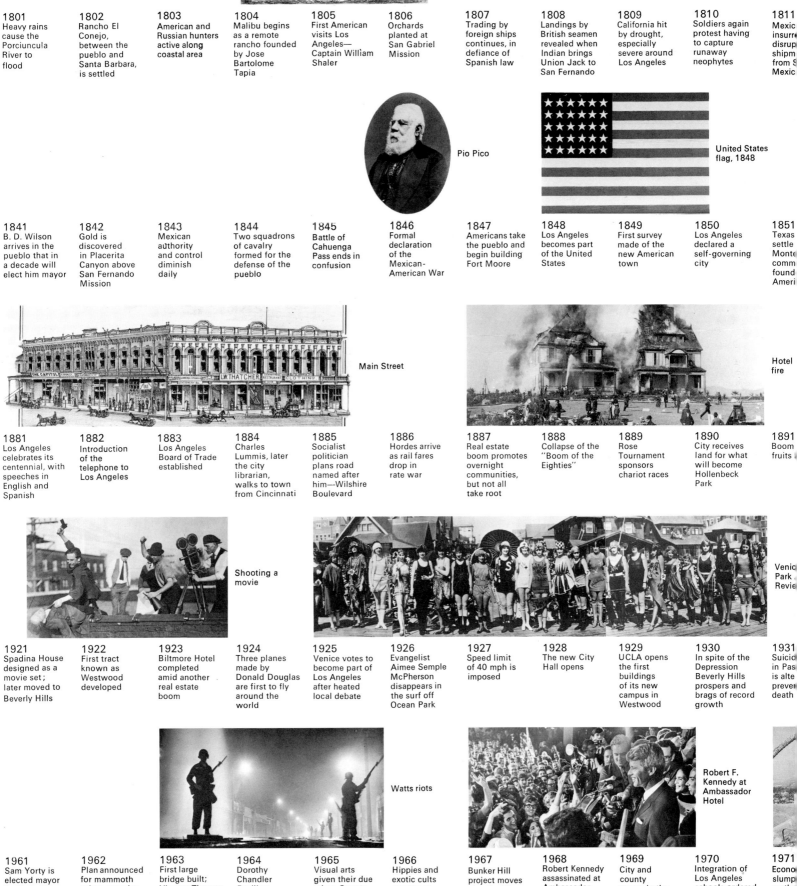

1781

Governor Felipe de Neve establishes a settlement dedicated to the Queen of Angels

The humble colonists, led by Spanish soldiers, came up from Mexico by boat, mule, horse, and foot. They were poor and had nothing to lose, but hoped to gain a new life in Alta California.

Felipe de Neve was governor of the Californias, then under Spanish control. As early as 1777, he had proclaimed Monterey as the capital of the New World north of Mexico. A settlement was started at San Jose later that year. The second civil settlement, near Rio Porciuncula, would eventually become Los Angeles.

The Spanish government promised volunteers who were willing to make the long trek north a salary of ten pesos a month plus rations. Governor Neve was looking for twenty-four families but only fourteen applied. Two of those families quit before the journey began, and another dropped out along the way when a child was stricken by smallpox. The eleven remaining families traveled more than eight months to reach their new home.

Corporal Jose Vicente Feliz led the founding party from San Gabriel Mission to El Pueblo de Nuestra Senora la Reina de Los Angeles de Porciuncula (the Town of Our Lady the Queen of the Angels of Porciuncula). Of the eleven founding fathers two were Spaniards, four Indians, two blacks, two mulattoes, and one mestizo. The accompanying wives were mulattoes or Indians.

The townsite had been chosen and laid out by Governor Neve, a remarkable administrator who realized that the fledgling community would need water and protection from the wind. He designed a plaza, 200 feet wide by 300 feet long, with building lots for the settlers, a large space set aside for a church, and surrounding land for agriculture. Mules, mares, cows, calves, sheep, and goats were distributed to the colonists. The new life began.

Statue of the founding father overlooking the Los Angeles Plaza

A priest precedes the pueblo

In 1782 Father Junipero Serra visited the new settlement as well as San Gabriel Mission. Serra was no stranger to these parts. He had left his post as professor of philosophy at Mallorca to come to the New World. In 1769 Serra and Captain Gaspar de Portola led a small group of friars from Mexico to the Californias. The priest helped found San Gabriel Mission in 1771, ten years before the settlement of Los Angeles. During his visit in 1782 he expelled three families from El Pueblo de Nuestra Senora la Reina de Los Angeles for shirking their community duties.

Statue of Father Junipero Serra at the Plaza

Missions of colonialism

Church and state worked hand in hand in the Californias. Catholic missionaries wanted to save the souls of the "heathen" Indians to the north. Spanish authorities wanted to secure bases in the Californias in order to promote trade and control territory that was open to Russian forays from the north. Franciscan padres and Spanish soldiers together led the early expeditions out of Mexico northward into the Californias.

El Pueblo de Nuestra Senora la Reina de Los Angeles was at first just a tiny commercial outpost for Spain and a struggling enclave of support for army presidios and missionary padres. No one—not even the farsighted Neve—dreamed of Los Angeles as a potential paradise. Rainfall was rare and life seemed forever dependent on the vicissitudes of the waters of the Porciuncula. Padres and pobladores (settlers) had come to a land where survival would demand struggle, sacrifice, and even heroics.

Cannon at San Gabriel Mission

1784

The lure of the land

Los Angeles was only three years old when soldiers stationed in the area began to ask for land grants. One of the first applicants was Jose Manuel Nieto, who requested a "grazing place situated at three leagues distance" from San Gabriel Mission. He promised "not to harm a living soul" and pledged respect for the friars nearby as well as for the settlers in town. Governor Pedro Fages, Neve's successor, granted the request provided that Nieto promise not to harm either the "pagan Indians" or the inhabitants of the Spanish enclaves. Nieto's holdings eventually increased to 167,000 acres—the beginnings of the ranchos and a foretaste of what would become Los Angeles sprawl.

A contemporary tract development at Walnut

1785

Weapons among the angels

The pueblo was a simple community, an agricultural enclave dedicated to growing corn, peppers, and grapes. San Gabriel Mission supplied the spiritual guidance for the small community; the military base—as well as government headquarters—was at the Santa Barbara presidio, a Spanish garrison.

No community cut off from Mexico could survive without security. Approximately 4,000 Indians lived in the immediate area. They seemed peaceful enough, but the colonists were uncertain and uneasy. Yuma Indians along the Colorado River had killed a Spanish expeditionary force the same year the Los Angeles pueblo was founded. The ignorant and illiterate pobladores were afraid of "heathens" they neither knew nor understood.

Just to play safe, 35 pounds of gunpowder and 800 bullets were sent to Los Angeles in 1785.

The irony became apparent later when the missions rather than ammunition were responsible for the demise of the docile Indians. The native culture was destroyed as Indians moved into San Gabriel to become converts and workers. Never having been exposed to the diseases of a "civilized" people, Indians died of afflictions such as measles and syphilis carried by Spanish soldiers. Indian deaths outnumbered Indian births even as San Gabriel grew.

There was a cruel irony in the friendliness that the Indians showed to the settlers from the beginning. Father Francisco Palou, Serra's biographer, innocently noted: "The sight of the image of Our Lady produced a wonderful change upon the gentiles [pagans] surrounding the Mission of San Gabriel, and they came very often to visit the friars, seemingly not able to sufficiently express their joy that they should have come to live among them, and the desire to show their gratitude by their good will and their presents." As the pueblo at Los Angeles prospered, the Gabrielino Indians began to disappear.

A modern cache of confiscated weapons, including old swords and new rifles, collected by the Los Angeles County sheriff's department for melting

1786

Settlers take title

Governor Pedro Fages gave the pobladores full title to their lots at the Plaza. Each of the founding families marked the formal document with the sign of the Holy Cross, because none of the settlers could write. When the town was first settled, the lots were apportioned by a drawing. Families could build and farm the allotted parcels as tenants, but they did not become legal owners until 1786.

Fages had been a lieutenant with Portola during early expeditions to the Californias and returned to govern as Neve's successor. He brought along his wife and their two children; no previous ranking official had risked taking command with family in tow. The settlers had become landowners, the soldiers were receiving land grants, and the governor could enjoy his personal life in a remote station. Los Angeles was beginning to acquire some of the comforts—and courtesies—of home.

Aerial view of the Palos Verdes Peninsula

1787

Local government comes to Los Angeles

Corporal Jose Vicente Feliz, one of the original military escorts from Mexico, was appointed comisionado of the Los Angeles pueblo by Governor Fages. A comisionado served as a kind of presiding judge, community arbitrator, and father figure—the first local government official in the settlement, reporting to his superiors at the Santa Barbara presidio.

Feliz was the overseer of agriculture, the peacemaker in arguments between settlers, and the boss in matters of labor relations; he administered the employment and treatment of Indians who worked at the Plaza. Before he retired in 1800, Feliz was granted the land now known as the Silverlake area along with parcels of ground that later became Griffith Park, where a boulevard preserves his name.

New Americans, waiting to take the oath of citizenship, in front of the Los Angeles Music Center

*A founding father
becomes the first elected mayor*

Jose Vanegas, one of the original pobladores, was appointed alcalde, or mayor, of Los Angeles. The position involved more protocol than power; the alcalde was responsible to the comisionado, who in turn answered to Santa Barbara. But Los Angeles was beginning to produce its own leaders; when the people were allowed to select their own man in 1796, Vanegas was elected for a new term.

The very first alcalde was an Indian from Mexico as was his wife, Maria Bonifacia Maxima Aguilar. When they made the trek north in 1781, he was twenty-eight, she was twenty.

In 1973 Tom Bradley became the first black mayor of a major American city with a predominantly white population. He had been an athlete at UCLA, a Los Angeles policeman, a city councilman, and an attorney before his election to the highest local office.

Los Angeles mayor Tom Bradley, dressed as an alcalde

*Government grows
some more grass roots*

The first Los Angeles governing officials, appointed to serve with Alcalde Vanegas, were called regidores. Felipe Garcia and Manuel Camero assumed the honors, helping the comisionado and the alcalde resolve local disputes.

Today the City Council of Los Angeles is composed of fifteen men and women, each representing a different section of the city. The Los Angeles County Board of Supervisors numbers five, each representing about 1.5 million citizens. While the council has legislative power within the city, the board has legislative, executive, and even quasi-judicial power over a county covering more than 4,000 square miles.

Los Angeles County Board of Supervisors—from left, Baxter Ward, Pete Schabarum, Yvonne Brathwaite Burke, Kenneth Hahn, and Edmund Edelman

A body count at the turn of the decade

In its first census, in 1790, the new community could count 141 noses, an almost threefold increase from the original population of 44 members in 11 families. Indians were not counted in the first census; they did not own land in Spanish terms and were not considered gente de razon—that is, civilized people.

Population grew steadily but slowly every ten years. Spanish soldiers retired from military duty to become local ranchers. Families increased. The population of Los Angeles exceeded 1,000 before the census of 1840. Yet by 1850 there were only 1,610 people. American statehood and new overland settlers boosted the population to 4,399 by 1860. The first big land boom echoed in the 1880s, and a hundred years after the first census Los Angeles could boast a population of 50,395.

Home of Peace Memorial Park in East Los Angeles

Grain production— a growing business

Los Angeles continued to grow and prosper—quietly, very quietly. Even Hubert Howe Bancroft, California's consummate collector of historical material for whom Bancroft Library was named, had little to say about this period. He called the 1790s the decade when practically nothing happened in the sleepy pueblo of Los Angeles.

In 1791 there were twenty-nine dwellings in the town plus a chapel, guardhouse, administrative buildings, and granaries. All were made of adobe and surrounded by a thick adobe wall.

Grain production was becoming a big business; the equable climate, healthful for crops as well as for humans, enabled the pueblo to produce more grain than any of the nine existing missions, except for San Gabriel Mission up the trail.

Present-day barley harvest in Antelope Valley

The young pueblo— a haven for the retired

Governor Arrillaga complained in 1792, "If it were not for the invalids, Los Angeles would not amount to anything." Of the 141 people included in the first census of the pueblo, only nine were beyond middle age. But that soon changed. Spanish soldiers stayed in California after retiring from the military. There they found land and warmth and an opportunity to define one's own life—attractive advantages that persist.

The city would one day become a health haven, advertising juicy oranges, a dry climate, and bountiful sunshine. For decades during the pre-smog years before World War II, older people migrated to Los Angeles because they realized that its climate would be beneficial for their health.

Even though its skies have been hazed by smog, Los Angeles continues to lure; the Pomona lawn bowlers illustrate a continuing passion for an active old age in the sun.

(Overleaf) Senior citizens exercise at Pomona Lawn Bowling Club

29

1793

*The first force organized
"to protect and serve"*

A small detachment of soldiers, under the comisionado's command, was sent from the presidio at Santa Barbara to protect the pueblo of Los Angeles. Another small group of soldiers and their families moved from the San Diego presidio to San Gabriel Mission.

The Spanish preferred that their California enclaves be nonviolent and not visited. They made every effort to keep the peace in their settlements and to keep strangers out of them. English explorer George Vancouver had hoped to take a look at Los Angeles in 1793 but was permitted to anchor his ship, *Discovery,* only at Santa Barbara and San Diego. After he passed the coast near Los Angeles, he noted: "A very advantageous settlement is established on a fertile spot somewhere in this neighborhood . . . called Pueblo de Los Angeles, 'the country town of the angels.' " Vancouver may have been the first English-speaking booster for Los Angeles who praised the pueblo without having seen it. Vague accounts such as Vancouver's are entered in the histories of the city because the people of the pueblo could not—or did not—keep records of their own.

*Los Angeles Police Academy
recruits work out at Elysian Park*

1794

*The mission, the military, and a
bit of sin*

The religious community at San Gabriel numbered about 1,000 neophytes by 1794. The term "neophyte" referred to a native Indian who came to the missions to be converted and stayed to do hard work in the fields. San Gabriel, administered by three padres and a small detachment of soldiers, had become the third largest mission of the chain in terms of population. A new stone church on the grounds was half completed, and agricultural yields were improving.

The relationships between the missionaries, soldiers, and neophytes, however, were far from ideal. Sometimes missionary zeal led to overworking the Indians, and at times the Indians fled. Soldiers assigned to bring back fugitive neophytes finally demanded that the friars do their own recapturing. The friars, displeased with military misbehavior—especially toward women neophytes—claimed that the soldiers were responsible for more sin than security. Conflict between church and state in southern California increased until the 1830s, when the missions were secularized under Mexican rule.

Interior of San Gabriel Mission

A pastoral place of plenty

The Spanish authorities worked hard to increase the amount of livestock raised in Los Angeles. As early as 1795 they knew that this quiet, pastoral region enjoyed an extraordinary agricultural promise.

That promise was fulfilled later, during the forty years between 1909 and 1949, when Los Angeles ranked as the number-one agricultural producer in the United States. Not until the 1950s, when orange trees were being bulldozed at the rate of one every fifty-five seconds and the groves gave way to housing tracts, did Los Angeles become truly urbanized. As recently as the late 1960s, Los Angeles, as a county, was still the largest livestock and dairy producer in the country; it also remained first in nursery and greenhouse output.

Today haystacks have been replaced by high-rise buildings. Most of the principal farming has moved into the neighboring counties of Ventura and Orange. Silos in Los Angeles are generally constructed of steel and glass, built to hold and store human beings. People tend to forget that this was once farmland; they are more apt to think of Los Angeles in terms of glamorous movie stars, lucrative oil strikes, and aerospace spectaculars. But ranching was what made this region and—for decades—fed the nation.

Hay bales in San Fernando Valley

The grain for Spain grew mostly on the plain

The largest crop of the decade, approximately 7,800 bushels, was harvested in 1796. Most of the yield was in maize, the remainder in wheat. During rich years of surplus, the Spanish sold grain at Santa Barbara or exported it from California by ship. Pack trains traveled the dirt trails between the Santa Barbara presidio and the Los Angeles breadbasket.

San Fernando Valley—between Santa Barbara and the pueblo—had ranchos as early as 1784, when Governor Fages granted Corporal Jose Maria Verdugo permission to move cattle onto ranges north of the town. Verdugo's Rancho San Rafael was on a sort of saddle between the Los Angeles River and the Arroyo Seco (dry gulch) at Pasadena, a grazing land that spread to the foothills of the area now called Eagle Rock.

The explorer Gaspar de Portola had discovered San Fernando Valley as early as 1769, while on an expedition with Father Juan Crespi. Crespi's diary describes a trek through present Sepulveda Pass during which the expeditionary party encountered a "large village of heathen, very friendly and docile," and they established the "newly discovered basin as Valley of Santa Catalina de Bononia de los Encinos." Encinos are oaks, and San Fernando Valley was once striped with them. Only a few remain.

Wheat harvest in Antelope Valley

A new mission marks the valley

The seventeenth California mission was established in September 1797, part of a chain that would expand to include twenty-one outposts of Christianity. Father Fermin Lasuen, Serra's successor, named the new mission San Fernando Rey de Espana, after Ferdinand III, a thirteenth-century Spanish king.

The first residents of San Fernando included two friars, three converted Indian families, and a military guard. As the mission grew, it set up an irrigation system, a winepress, tannery, smokehouse, carpenter shop, blacksmith shop, granaries, weaving room, and other enterprises necessary for a self-reliant community. The Indians living nearby were called Fernandenos, after the mission, just as the Indians who lived around San Gabriel had come to be known as Gabrielinos.

San Fernando Mission was an architectural improvement over bulky San Gabriel. The padres had discovered the beauty of arches below a red tile roof, low-slung proportions that would one day be the distinguishing elements of mission architecture and design. The setting was lush and luxuriant, a center of civilization set among vineyards and orchards in a vast plain of wild mustard. The mission, restored, still stands, but the neighborhood is decidedly less green.

Father Fermin Lasuen, founder of San Fernando Mission

A criminal element emerges

The pueblo's first place of imprisonment was built during the tenure of Alcalde Guillermo Soto. Lack of obedience to local law may have become a growing problem. A place to hold runaway Indians must also have been an impetus to building a jail in town.

Real crime or violence between residents of Los Angeles did not become a major issue until after the Americans arrived in the middle of the nineteenth century, when the pueblo earned the dubious historical footnote of having formed California's first vigilance committee. After U.S. statehood was granted, there was a spate of murders, lynchings, bloody street fights, and public knifings, as well as an excess of thieves, crooked gamblers, Indian slave markets, and brothels. "Crime is perpetrated openly and with impunity," wrote the *Star,* the city's pioneer newspaper. Horace Bell arrived in town after the Gold Rush up north and bluntly noted: "There were more desperados in Los Angeles than in any place on the Pacific Coast . . . where the cutthroats of California and Mexico naturally met." Bell's book, *Reminiscences of a Ranger,* remains a classic tale of crime in Southern California. "The slightest misunderstandings," Bell stated, "were settled on the spot with knife or bullet, the Mexican preferring the former at close quarters and the American the latter."

In 1798 no one in the pueblo would have predicted that this bucolic community, despite its new jail, would become in little more than fifty years a sore spot of mayhem and massacre.

(Overleaf) Los Angeles County Jail

Adobe and a dignity a-growing

By the end of the eighteenth century the pueblo had thirty adobe houses; none of the dwellings of 1799 remains today. The oldest house in town is the Avila Adobe, built in 1818, repaired in 1930, and restored again in recent years. The Avila is on Olvera Street, where the annual Las Posadas parade celebrates the journey of Joseph and Mary into Bethlehem.

Adobe, sun-dried bricks of clay often mixed with straw and manure, was a practical building material for a city with limited tools and manufacturing ability. Adobe was thick; it remained relatively cool in summer and retained heat in winter. The first pre-adobe houses were much humbler, hand-built huts of willow branches tied together with reeds from the river. Roofs, which were made of thick and claylike mud, were subject to cracks and collapse.

Today a Mexican marketplace and tourist attraction, Olvera Street is exactly where the pueblo began, directly above the original water supply from the Porciuncula—now the Los Angeles River. The modern remaking of Olvera Street began in the late 1920s, when Mrs. Christine Sterling bullied the city fathers into using prison labor to rebuild and restore the city's birthplace.

Annual Las Posadas
pre-Christmas procession along
Olvera Street

A welcome increase of animals

At the turn of the century the population of settlers numbered only 315, while horses and cattle were increasing at a much faster rate. From 1791 to 1800 the cattle and horse count in Los Angeles went from 3,000 to 12,500, the largest livestock increase anywhere in California.

Horses were the mainstay of local transit. The carreta, a wooden cart pulled by two oxen, was a slow alternative to travel on horseback. The trails connecting the community to presidios, missions, and ranchos were primitive and difficult. Under Spanish rule seven land grants for grazing had been issued for fields around the pueblo. These grants became the ranchos, measured in varas (nearly one yard).

Owners rode around their properties on horseback, roughly calculating varas by lengths of a lariat. More precise was each landholder's promise to build and occupy a house within one year of obtaining the land grant. He also agreed to cultivate the soil, introduce more livestock, and construct a corral. Like the missions, ranchos were forced to become self-sufficient compounds because of the distances between settlements and the rough connecting trails.

Horses grazing at Calabasas

1801

*Rainfall, a precious
rarity, a sometime danger*

Carey McWilliams wrote in *Southern California Country* that "there was never a region so unlikely to become a vast metropolitan area as Southern California. It is . . . man-made, a gigantic improvisation."

Water was the precious reason for settling at the Plaza in the first place. The Porciuncula River made planting possible on an otherwise arid plain. Rain was rare, but when it came, floods were almost certain to follow. Comedian Carl Reiner would later offer a wry observation: "When it rains in New York, people get wet. When it rains in Southern California, people get killed."

The Los Angeles River was dammed early in the nineteenth century by the padres at San Gabriel; they wanted to store the water, when it ran, for the next dry season. The settlers were furious; they wanted the full run past the zanja madre (mother ditch) for their fields. If the friars and soldiers fought over administration of Indians, the friars and colonists fought over access to water. Thirst continues today: Los Angeles imports water from northern California and the Colorado River through hundreds of miles of pipes, gigantic supply systems just to keep the faucets running.

*Downtown Los Angeles
during a deluge*

1802

Hard going between the government and the governed

At the beginning of the century the crude trail running from Santa Barbara—the seat of the government—to the village of Los Angeles remained primitive. But the land between had already become valuable.

Jose Polanco and Ignacio Rodriguez were allowed to move onto Rancho El Conejo in 1802. They shared ownership of the territory during their lifetimes. Polanco died without heirs, but Rodriguez left a wife and children. The Polanco portion of El Conejo was claimed by Don Jose Antonio de la Guerra, an officer at Santa Barbara and an aristocrat, born in Spain. For fourteen years Rodriguez's daughter, Dona Maria del Carmen, fought Guerra's occupation of El Conejo. A Mexican governor would later have to divide Rancho El Conejo in half, marking new boundaries and separating two families.

The Stagecoach Inn at Newbury Park today is a museum, situated along the Ventura Freeway in old Conejo country. It opened as the Grand Union Hotel in 1876, a resting place between Santa Barbara and Los Angeles. It was moved in 1964 to accommodate the freeway and was rebuilt after a fire in 1970.

Historic Stagecoach Inn at Newbury Park, between Santa Barbara and Los Angeles

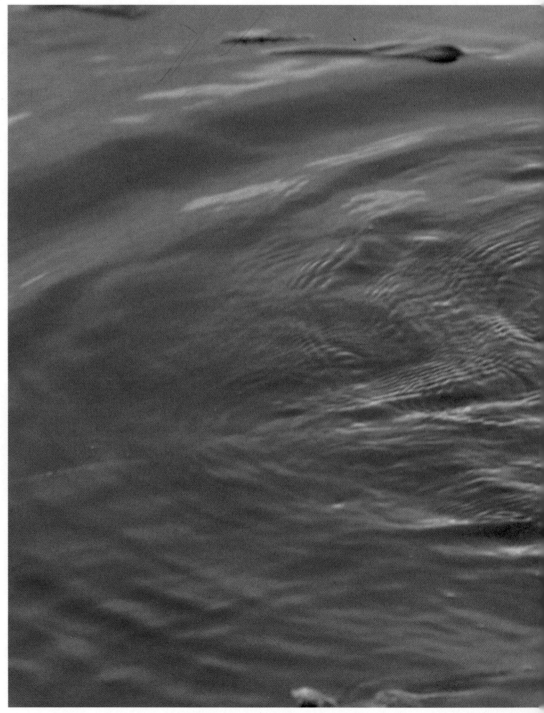

44

1803

After the otter, a fur piece

Americans and Russians from Alaska were sailing down the California coast in the early 1800s, hunting seal and sea otter for their valuable pelts. Despite Spanish prohibitions against foreign incursions, ships were able to drop hunters ashore at Santa Catalina and other Channel Islands off the southern California coast. American Jonathan Winship, captain of the *O'Cain,* suggested a joint venture in 1803 with a group of Russian-sponsored Aleutian hunters.

Experts today have estimated that between 1741 and 1911 over 200,000 otters along the California and Baja California coast were killed for their skins. This mammal, a member of the weasel family, was almost extinct by the beginning of the twentieth century. An international treaty in 1911 offered some protection to the sea otter. A California law in 1913 brought additional protection, and in 1941 a refuge was established near Carmel.

Sea otters, which feed on abalone, sea urchins, and clams, now number about 2,000 along the California coast. The population is drifting southward again, as close to Los Angeles as Malibu. Even while the Carmel-based Friends of the Sea Otter works to expand protection, Pismo Beach clammers are in fierce competition with the mammal because of its appetite for shellfish.

Sea otters cavort along the California coast

1804

A man to own the Malibu

Jose Bartolome Tapia came to California in 1775, long before Los Angeles was settled. In 1786 his father, Felipe, brought the family to San Jose, the earliest pueblo in California. Jose moved down to San Luis Obispo a few years later to oversee a mission rancho. He married, moved to Los Angeles, and helped work the lands of Jose Manuel Nieto, one of the first land grant recipients.

Tapia knew how to farm, how to keep cattle, how to haul produce from a remote rancho to town. He applied for his own land, a beautiful twenty-two-mile stretch of coast with canyons, mountains, and marine terraces. In 1802 or 1804—accounts conflict—Santa Barbara granted him his land, the most remote rancho in the area. Rancho Topanga, Malibu y Sequit took part of its name from the Chumash Indian village of Maliwu, which once thrived along the creek.

Buying and selling Malibu began in 1848 when Leon Victor Prudhomme, a twenty-six-year-old Frenchman, bought the land from the Tapia heirs for 400 pesos. In 1857 Don Mateo Keller from Los Angeles paid ten cents an acre for the Prudhomme property. Before the turn of the century Keller sold Malibu to Frederick Hastings Rindge for ten dollars an acre.

May K. Rindge became "queen of the Malibu" after her husband died in 1905. She decided to keep the rancho intact, to resist state roadways, the Southern Pacific Railroad, and all public intrusion. She built fences, sponsored armed patrols, and fought holding actions all the way to the U.S. Supreme Court.

But Malibu could not remain remote. It would one day become the favorite weekend retreat of the movie colony, the secluded refuge for rock 'n' roll stars, the rich strand for real estate speculation. Malibu today has fires, fierce waves, and fishermen; it also has Pepperdine University, shopping centers, and condominiums. A house with an ocean view on one of Keller's ten-cent acres now sells for at least $500,000.

Malibu is where modern settlers come to fish and find the good life

1805

The Americans are coming

Captain William Shaler was one of the earliest visitors from the United States when he sailed the *Lelia Byrd* into Los Angeles waters. In 1805 Shaler was coming back from the Hawaiian Islands, loaded with tales of whaling and shark hunting and enthusiasm for the potentials of Pacific trade. He sailed home for New England with more stories about the little settlement at Los Angeles and the riches to be made from the pelts of the sea otters off the Channel Islands.

So began American trade with Alta California, in spite of the Spanish penalty for doing business with foreign-ers, which was loss of property and death. Ships anchored at Santa Catalina and sent small boats to the mainland. Manufactured goods from New England were smuggled into Los Angeles in return for furs and, later, hides and tallow. Freebooting enterprise had arrived. The otters have not returned to Catalina, but visiting yachts are there every weekend, basking off the coast of a Los Angeles County nature conservancy covering sixty-six square miles.

Buffalo graze above yacht harbor at Catalina Island

1806

The start of sweet juices

Father Jose Maria Zalvidea at San Gabriel Mission was busy planting orchards in 1806. The fertility of the California soil for growing grapes, lemons, limes, peaches, pears, and apples was first exploited at the mission. Louis Vignes started the first orange grove in the pueblo a few years later. But the commercial fruit industry did not begin until 1841, when the American William Wolfskill came to town and planted a two-acre orange grove. Those two acres were expanded to grow 2,500 trees, once the largest orange-tree stand in the United States.

Population crowds out peaches and oranges today. But in 1806 the major problem was the swarms of locusts that destroyed whole crops of corn, beans, and peas.

(Overleaf) Peach-picking time at Little Rock

49

1807

Foreign vessels cruise the coast

Captains from several countries followed in the wake of Shaler's visit. By 1807 the Spanish government was increasingly concerned about uninvited vessels sailing up and down the coast.

The international smugglers liked the coves and caves around the Palos Verdes Peninsula, across the channel from Catalina, as suitable spots to dump or store contraband. San Pedro, next to Palos Verdes, was the primary port, a place sailors called the Hell of California because of its rocks and steep cliffs.

California had been discovered by the outside world, and it would not for long remain a sleepy little farming community for Spain.

Cruise ship Pacific Princess, *out of London, leaving Los Angeles Harbor*

1808

Now the British are coming

In August 1808 a converted Indian arrived at San Fernando Mission with a peculiar piece of colored material. He said a ship captain had given it to him up the coast. The friars consulted the government; the fabric was an English flag. A new instance of foreign intrusion—the British were taking riches out of Alta California.

Alta California brought in British riches in 1967, when the city of Long Beach bought the *Queen Mary,* perhaps the most famous passenger liner ever built. The *Queen Mary* carried the affluent across the oceans before World War II and carried the military across the Atlantic during the war. But jet aircraft made the luxury liner obsolete in the 1960s. Looking for a tourist attraction to compete with movie studios in Los Angeles and Disneyland in Anaheim, Long Beach purchased the liner as a hotel, museum, and local landmark. The English flag flies daily.

The Queen Mary, *bought from Britain, at permanent berth in Long Beach*

1809

A dry spell, one of many

Drought came to California in 1809 and has returned repeatedly—most recently with the fearsome dry spell of 1976–77, when the whole state wondered whether the rains would ever return. Drought always brings human uneasiness and guilt along with parched earth. In 1809 the Los Angeles comisionado said that gambling, drunkenness, and "other excesses" were "alarmingly on the increase."

In 1977, before the downpours of December began, Los Angeles residents were installing water-saving devices in their showers, toilets, and kitchen sinks. Suddenly the modern settlers had to learn not to hose down driveways, not to irrigate during sunshine hours, not to run their washing machines with less than full loads. One nervous Malibu resident even filled his swimming pool with earth rather than keep it filled with precious water.

Garden green is an induced color in Los Angeles. The natural state is brush brown. After the spring rains have ceased, the hills annually turn from green to brown to blanched gold.

The sun-cracked desert of Antelope Valley

First the Indians lost ground, then freedom

The soldiers, settlers, and padres continued to argue over water rights and Indian recapture. By 1810 the military cadres at San Gabriel and San Fernando were protesting having to make biweekly forays into the field to capture and return Indian runaways.

The Gabrielino and Fernandeno tribes were in decline. The arrival of the whites brought oppression rather than divine revelation to the Indians. The anthropologist A. L. Kroeber later wrote about the way the missions "broke their spirit." People who once lived off the land now found their land crowded by cattle and competing crops, all introduced by the new settlers. When the Indians moved into the missions for "salvation," they could not accept the regimentation imposed by the friars. Indian women practiced crude abortion rather than reproduce more workers for the fields. When they tried to escape by running away, the Indians could not evade the soldiers sent out on horseback. When they moved into Los Angeles, they could not avoid being exploited.

Present-day Los Angeles has an Indian population, but the contemporary Indians all come from faraway tribes. Not a single Gabrielino or Fernandeno descendant survives.

Indian wickiups at Los Angeles County Arboretum

Anguish at the gates of Angeltown

Spain was having its own troubles when the decade began. Napoleon I had already deposed Ferdinand VII and installed Joseph Bonaparte, his brother, as king. With France attempting to take over the Iberian Peninsula, the Spanish had little time or money for Mexico and California. Spanish vessels stopped making their usual calls to the Pacific coast by 1811. Spanish payments to soldiers in the colonies and Spanish supplies were cut.

In Mexico there were cries for insurrection and independence. In little Los Angeles the Spanish soldiers had to turn to the missions for support and supplies. Smuggling increased along the coast; more Americans sailed in and out carrying increased amounts of contraband. The way to survive hard times was to sail around diminished Spanish authority. Settlers cashed their crops wherever they could. Ferdinand eventually recovered the throne, but Spain never regained control over California.

Protesters on the march for work at Paramount Pictures

1812

*An earthquake
to make times tougher*

The earthquakes of 1812 shook Alta California from San Diego to Santa Barbara. At San Juan Capistrano, south of Los Angeles, the quake on December 8 occurred during early morning mass. The vaulted roof of the mission church collapsed, killing more than three dozen worshipers. The same quake wrecked the church tower at San Buenaventura north of Los Angeles.

The quake on December 21 destroyed La Purisima Church at Santa Barbara and almost wrecked the church at San Luis Obispo. That year came to be known as the "Year of the Earthquakes," after the succession of shakes that caused adobe buildings to tumble throughout the region.

Quakes came to Los Angeles in later years and continued into the twentieth century, nurturing that not-so-fantastic fantasy of a city that would one day quake, shake, and break away from the rest of the United States.

Downtown Crocker Bank in simulated earthquake

Hard times become harder

Hard times become harder

Revolution was spreading throughout Mexico by 1813. The Spanish soldiers stationed around Los Angeles were cut off from their salaries and supplies. Some people were destitute in California; almost everyone was discontented.

The Spanish, disturbed by continuing disputes between the military and the missionaries, wanted to secularize the missions. Spain had originally intended the missions to be a strong civilizing influence as well as a means of controlling the colony; ten years after their founding, the missions were to merge into a larger community, with the neophytes becoming free citizens. But the missionaries, benefiting from free land and free Indian labor, resisted. Since the missions were producing the food to sustain Alta California during these hard times, effective secularization, under Mexican rule, would have to wait until two decades and dozens of disturbances had come and gone.

The modern church-sponsored missions along Los Angeles's Main Street are still in the business of saving souls, converting alcoholics rather than Indians. Salvation is rare, but the missions do offer food and bed for otherwise destitute drinkers.

Skid Row—a modern meaning for missions

1814

Cattle and a cornerstone

The cornerstone was laid for a church at the Plaza in 1814. Initial funding came from the sale of barrels of brandy, donated by the missionaries. The first church in the pueblo, a small adobe built in 1784, was no longer large enough to hold the settlers. The new church would be a toast to the grapes grown at San Gabriel. But the brandy ran out and the project was postponed.

Meanwhile Don Antonio Maria Lugo had permission to graze his cattle on

Rancho San Antonio, between the Los Angeles and San Gabriel rivers. Lugo's father had been part of the original military escort at the founding of the pueblo. Don Antonio, a stern man who always rode with a sword strapped against his saddle, would serve five terms as alcalde of the city. The Lugos were a proud and prominent family until the mid-nineteenth century, when two of Don Antonio's grandsons were accused of murdering two Yankee teamsters and were almost lynched when relations between Americans and Spanish-speaking Californians deteriorated into mob violence.

The cattle at Pierce College today are part of an extensive program in agriculture and animal husbandry, rural reminders in the midst of urban development.

Cattle graze at Pierce College, in San Fernando Valley, next to an industrial park

1815

The rains came—and kept coming
Precious water turned into rampant peril as rain fell for ten straight days and nights. The Los Angeles River grew from trickle to torrent, splashing over the Plaza, soaking homes, and again proving the unpredictability of nature in what is normally a dry sun-drenched place.

When the rains outdo themselves in Los Angeles, streets become lagoons, canyons become catch basins, and hills begin to slide. The land has always been as shifting as the culture. In the hills shale, a common rock in the substrata, absorbs water, which acts as a lubricant; then the laminated rocks begin to slip, one upon another, and not infrequently a large hunk of hillside moves from one location to another. Such slides were serious enough in the adobe period, but today, with residences filling the canyons, whole neighborhoods have slipped down the Santa Monica Mountains into the flatlands below.

A landslide along Hollywood Freeway—a parking lot rolls onto driving lanes

1816

A mission flock evicted
In 1816 the missionaries at San Fernando were arguing with Patricio Pico, the owner of the surrounding land. Pico had advised the padres to keep their sheep off his grounds; the padres in turn informed him that they had no place else to graze them. The argument was typical. The missionaries had opposed private ownership of ranchlands even while the Spanish government was busy granting land to establish ranchos. The missions had grown up as self-contained communities; the government wanted the missions to serve settlements with food and faith, not to compete with them.

Even as Spanish control of the colonies was weakening because of conflicts in Spain, mission control of California was weakened by arguments about Indians, water rights, and grazing lands. The rancho owners were becoming powerful because they possessed the land.

The sheep population in Los Angeles County may have numbered more than 100,000 during the years of mission power; by 1854, after the missions' decline, the weekly *The Southern Californian* was complaining that there were no sheep left. A completely new sheep industry was reestablished a few years later.

(Overleaf) A herd of 800 sheep grazing at Calabasas in San Fernando Valley

63

1817

School starts, then recesses

Education enjoyed little priority in the pueblo. The settlers who struggled north from Mexico were themselves illiterate; they had none of the obsession for education that drove the New England colonists to build classrooms and set up regular curricula. School, in fact, was a potential threat to ranching. Children were needed out in the fields reaping, not reading books.

By Spanish order a school was opened by 1794 in San Jose, the first California settlement. San Diego and Santa Barbara also had schools. Los Angeles did not, until Governor Pablo Vicente de Sola ordered one to be built. Maximo Pina, a former soldier with a disability, was hired in 1817 to begin teaching. Sola wanted reading and writing emphasized in the lessons, but religious training seemed more important to the community; once children learned to read, all subsequent instruction was in religious matters. After he tried to teach for two years, at a salary equivalent to $140 a year, Pina left town, and the school closed. Education still had a low priority.

Historic one-room schoolhouse at Santa Paula just over the border in Ventura County

1818

A few constructive events

Work began again on a new Plaza Church in 1818. This time the citizens helped to fund construction with donations of cattle. Work continued until the government confiscated the cattle.

The Avila Adobe, oldest residence in town, was built on Olvera Street in 1818. That year Joseph Chapman, who became the first important American resident in Los Angeles, came to town. Chapman had been a privateer, sailing under Captain Hippolyte de Bouchard on the *Santa Rosa*. Bouchard was French by birth, but the *Santa Rosa* flew the Argentine flag; Argentina had already declared its independence from Spain and was sending ships up the Pacific coast to foment revolutions elsewhere. Chapman, second in command, went ashore at Monterey and was captured. Later he made his way south, but Don Antonio Maria Lugo, Los Angeles's alcalde, took him into custody and brought him to the pueblo.

Chapman was expert at felling the trees needed to build the Plaza Church. He later supervised the building of a gristmill at San Gabriel Mission. He became the best contractor in the city, eventually marrying a girl from Mexico, converting to Catholicism, and obtaining his own rancho up the coast near Ventura.

The restored Sepulveda House at the Plaza along Main Street; members of the Valadez, Gutierrez, Tapia, and Hallowell families— present-day Plaza merchants of Olvera Street—pose outside

1819

More trouble on troubled waters

Incidents at sea were increasing. The Bouchard expeditions had frightened the settlers in Los Angeles. After looting and pillaging at Monterey, where Chapman had been captured, two Bouchard vessels anchored off San Juan Capistrano, where the Argentine-inspired revolutionaries caused more havoc. Only a few years before, the Tarakanof pirates had been taken when a Russian trading vessel was intercepted at San Pedro; Captain Boris Tarakanof and twenty Aleutian sailors were the first foreign prisoners to be locked up in the Los Angeles jail, awaiting transfer to Santa Barbara.

Russian, English, and American privateers were cruising up and down the coast, preying on vessels and poaching from landing boats. Los Angeles requested additional troops and further protection in 1820. The Spanish government talked about sending twenty more soldiers to town, but they never arrived.

The U.S. Coast Guard cutter Point Camden, *on routine patrol off Los Angeles*

1820

Battles continue on land

Even as insecurity spread along the coastline, disputes between the padres and pueblo ranchers continued. In 1820 it was San Gabriel Mission's turn to protest. Father Jose Maria Zalvidea complained because friends and relatives of the Los Angeles comisionado insisted on grazing their stock on mission land.

Zalvidea was responsible for San Gabriel becoming the wealthiest of the California missions. He had planted the vineyards, established the soap works, started the tannery, and organized the spinning. He sternly managed the Indi-

an labor force; unmarried Indian women were separated from the men and forced to live like nuns. Yet he was generous to travelers and visitors. Ranchero Don Hugo Perfecto Reid later summed up the Zalvidea administration: "Everything under him was organized and that organization kept up with the lash." But Zalvidea was beginning to lose control during these troubled years; even his glorious gardens were being overrun by livestock and trampled by trespassers.

A field of poppies in Antelope Valley

Remaking the mother ditch

By 1821 the settlers were busy digging a new aqueduct, a zanja madre, from the Los Angeles River into town; recurrent drought followed by deluge and consequent destruction convinced the community to reconstruct its water supply. Progress was slow, partly because most of the workers were unpaid; citizens volunteered to help with the digging during their spare time.

By the 1970s Southern California's appetite for energy and water had become awesome. The Castaic program, billed by its sponsors as "one of the largest pumped storage hydroelectric projects in the world," utilizes water from the California aqueduct to generate more than 1.2 million kilowatts of electricity. The Los Angeles Department of Water and Power shares output with the California Department of Water Resources in this $450 million section of a vast network of power-producing, field-irrigating installations stretching the length of the state.

Massive pipes of the Castaic Power Project north of San Fernando Valley

Mexico proclaims independence from Spain, and California pledges allegiance to Mexico

Word traveled slowly. California found out about the Mexican revolution six months after it happened. Although none of the California settlements had participated in the separation from Spain, Governor Pablo Vicente de Sola and his council decided to recognize the new Mexican empire. Cannons were fired in Monterey, a priest blessed Mexican independence, and there were appropriate fiestas to celebrate Los Angeles's new loyalty.

The presidios and settlements in California were entitled to send representatives to Mexico; the delegate from Los Angeles was Jose Palomares, who later was accused of harboring anti-American sentiments during the turbulent period at mid-century when California switched allegiance from Mexico to the United States.

Flags changed at the Plaza; down came the lion of Spain, up went the serpent of Mexico. A treasurer and a secretary were added to the local government in Los Angeles, now called the ayuntamiento, or municipal council. Flags and fiestas aside, the revolution hardly touched life in the little city.

(Overleaf) A performance of Ballet Folklorico de Mexico

A new church at the Plaza, completed at last

The church at the Plaza, under construction for five years, underfinanced by brandy and cattle, was finally finished as Los Angeles's Mexican period began. The first church at the Plaza was built in 1784. After the settlers outgrew it, a second church was planned in 1814, and a cornerstone was laid. But the heavy rains of 1815 flooded the site, and the new church was moved uphill. Dedication ceremonies were held in 1822 even though the building was unfinished. There were no floor and no seats. A borrowed bell from San Gabriel called the congregation to worship.

Located at the head of the Plaza with houses flanking it on smaller plots, the church was the centerpiece of the city. The present Plaza Church, restored and expanded, stands at Sunset and Main.

Saint Basil's Church, designed by A. C. Martin with sculpted windows by Claire Falkenstein, stands at Wilshire and Kingsley, concrete witness to modernity and the eventual westward movement of the city.

Saint Basil's Roman Catholic Church on Wilshire Boulevard, built in 1974

Social standing and social slippage

From the beginning the warm weather and easy ways of Los Angeles attracted the rootless, the shiftless, the helpless. In 1824 the alcalde received complaints about vagrants loitering and littering in town. With Spanish restrictions gone, trading ships were arriving from all over the world. Luxuries were being imported in exchange for hides, but derelicts were also arriving. For better and worse the little pueblo was becoming part of the larger world. The officials sent up from Mexico were not repressive; they were also not very effective. Local landowners began wearing fancy gold-braided clothes and going about their business with little regard for Mexican authority or municipal responsibility.

Modern Los Angeles likes to brag about being a mobile society, where ability and ambition mean more than ancestral names. Lack of caste and class places a premium on individual effort; lack of snobbery allows easy entry for newcomers. There is truth in that brag.

Skid Row—next to the Civic Center

A river reroutes itself

In 1825 the unpredictable Los Angeles River flooded, overflowing its banks downtown. It changed its course again, merging with the San Gabriel River to empty at the port of San Pedro. The waters once meandered westward in a series of swamps and sloughs, eventually emptying into Ballona Creek at Playa del Rey. The new route sliced south, generally marking the concrete channel of today.

The old Ballona Creek would become the world's largest small-craft harbor, a Los Angeles County creation of the 1960s. Marina del Rey shelters approximately 6,000 boats, more than 12,000 permanent residents, and has about 10,000 apartments—desirable homes for single swingers and sometime sailors. Marina critics call it plastic, the ultimate Southern California put-down. Indeed the county once did plant plastic trees along the northern border of the project to ensure a permanent green. The trees were eventually replaced, but the plastic image persists. Marina people nevertheless go about their pleasures without missing a mai tai or a happy hour.

Marina del Rey, a man-made yacht harbor where the Los Angeles River used to meet the sea, seen from the Goodyear blimp

First of the overland Americans

Jedediah Strong Smith, leader of fifteen fur trappers, plodded his way from Utah over mountains, across the Mojave Desert, and into the San Gabriel Mission. He was the first pioneer American to come to Los Angeles by land.

He was not exactly welcome. The governor refused to permit his passage northward along the coast. The party had to wend its way back to the Great Salt Lake, battling blizzards in the Sierra Nevada. But Smith returned the next year, surviving an Indian massacre, loss of his horses, and a lack of food. He still was not welcome. One account claims that the government accused the trappers of being spies and that only American sea captains were able to persuade the authorities that the Smith party was harmless.

Those were troubled days. The elections of 1826 were overturned as illegal and had to be repeated. The town government passed new laws against gambling, prostitution, and blasphemy. Smuggling continued to be big business at Catalina Island.

(Overleaf) Downtown Harbor Freeway, everyday arrival route for overland commuters

Gardens amid growing disorder

In 1827 Auguste Duhault-Cilly, a visitor from France, arrived in Los Angeles. He counted eighty-two houses in Los Angeles, noted that the gardens around those houses were well cultivated—almost his only affirmative comment—and complained about an alarming lack of municipal order. The alcalde, he noted, was unable to assure protection of private property. The smugglers were coming; the Yankees were arriving; the Mexican government was feeble and far away.

The site of the well-cultivated Rose Gardens at Exposition Park was a private racetrack and fairgrounds in the 1870s. After the racetrack–fairgrounds went bankrupt, the city, county, and state purchased the property in joint tenancy in 1898; landscape architect Wilber Cook, Jr., was hired to design the gardens in 1911. The gardens, which cover seven acres between the University of Southern California and the Memorial Coliseum and are flanked by state and county museums, now boast 16,000 bushes representing 165 varieties of roses—the biggest such patch in the world, a spectacular free tourist attraction which reaches a peak of splendor in spring.

Rose Gardens at Exposition Park

1828

Shipwrecks and streetlights

Americans arrived at the pueblo in a variety of ways, some quite dramatic. When the brig *Danube* was wrecked at San Pedro in 1828, several members of the crew came ashore to take up permanent residence. John Temple came from Massachusetts by safer ship, formed a partnership with George Rice, and opened the first general store. Abel Stearns, another Massachusetts merchant, arrived by way of Mexico and became a prominent landholder and legislator.

These new arrivals were subject to odd rules and regulations of the young community. For example, to combat the dark and disorder—while sparing the city any expense—owners of more than two rooms facing a main thoroughfare were ordered to hang a lighted lantern at their residential doors during the evening, from twilight to night. Presumably Los Angeles pulled in its sidewalks after nightfall.

A modern victim of poor visibility, the *Dominator* was wrecked in 1961, having hit a reef in the fog off Palos Verdes Peninsula. Pieces of the *Dominator* are still stranded on the coastal rocks.

The once-good ship Dominator, *aground off Palos Verdes*

Drought accompanies disruption
Mexican authority was tested in 1829 when Joaquin Solis led a band of revolutionaries against the government in Santa Barbara. A group of volunteers left Los Angeles to help suppress the insurrection and restore order. Such disruption was occurring with increased frequency.

Meanwhile drought had returned: 1827 was a dry year, as was 1828 and 1829. Cattle died on the plains by the thousands; their hides were stripped and sold, small compensation for loss of crops and livestock. Residents were depressed by the apparent collapse of the government and by the harsh caprices of nature.

In our time protest marches against the government have become routine since the 1960s, replete with regular lines of march, police monitors, and placards especially designed for media coverage. Most contemporary political protests in Los Angeles are orderly, unlike the revolutionary escapades of the nineteenth century.

Chicano protest march downtown on Sixth Street

Demand for hide and tallow but no dairy
Despite drought, cattle had increased to 40,000 head by the turn of the decade. Livestock was big business, the exchange commodity for merchandise brought into San Pedro from all over the world.

The Scottish merchant Alexander Forbes, who was a student of cattle raising in the Los Angeles area, was appalled at the marginal use of the growing herds. He complained in his book *California:* "From this immense number of domestic animals, little advantage is obtained beyond the values of the hides and fat. The management of the dairy is totally unknown. There is hardly any such thing in use as butter and cheese, and what little is made is of the very worst description . . . execrable compounds of some coagulated milk and its cream mixed together."

Considering the strength of Forbes's complaints, no wonder some of the Anglos were not welcome in Los Angeles, even in the early days.

Julio de la Cruz, armed for work with a "stun gun" at a modern Los Angeles slaughterhouse

1831

Fresh traffic in trade

Jonathan Trumbull Warner was one of the first American trappers to settle in Los Angeles. Like many other Americans who came to pioneer and prosper, Warner assumed Spanish names—Don Juan J. Warner—and customs. He described the overland arrival of the William Wolfskill party from Santa Fe in 1831: "On their arrival in California they advantageously disposed of their blankets to the rancheros in exchange for mules. These New Mexicans mostly returned to Santa Fe . . . with the mules they had obtained in California. The appearance of these mules in New Mexico, owing to their large size, compared with those at the time used in the Missouri and Santa Fe trade . . . as well as the price at which they had been bought in barter for blankets, caused quite a sensation."

Trade between New Mexico and Los Angeles by pack animals flourished during the entire decade. Los Angeles was the principal California destination for pack trains and caravans and the point at which most of them converged. Today the modern four-level interchange is the central point at which the major freeways—Hollywood, Harbor, Pasadena—meet.

Four-level freeway interchange downtown, called the Stack

1832

Repression and a revolution

Chaos in Mexico spilled over into California. The empire in Mexico was transformed into a republic. Presidents were elected and ousted at the drop of a pistol. Don Manuel Victoria became the governor of California in 1831 and opted for despotism. He refused to let the legislature convene, abolished local governments, brought in troops, and banished those citizens who challenged his rule.

A band of anti-Victoria revolutionaries formed in San Diego and rode up to Los Angeles to foment insurrection—native Californians versus the governor appointed by Mexico. Don Jose Maria Avila (who had built the Plaza adobe in 1818) led the revolutionaries against Victoria. In hand-to-hand fighting Captain Romualdo Pacheco tried to protect Victoria from Avila's sword thrust but was himself killed. Avila was later shot and killed by a Mexican soldier, whereas Victoria, wounded, decided to abdicate and return to Mexico in 1832.

The bodies of Avila and Pacheco were brought to town for final rites. "Side by side, beneath the orange and the olive, in the little churchyard upon our Plaza, sleep the slayer and the slain," the American Stephen C. Foster wrote later.

Fort MacArthur, a major military debarkation center during World War II, is today a smaller installation near Los Angeles harbor.

Fort MacArthur at San Pedro, viewed from the air

1833

Unrest in the missions and the municipality

In 1833 the revolutionary government in Mexico made a declaration that the missions were to be secularized. Each Indian neophyte was to receive a share of land and stock. Government administrators would take charge, deposing the clergy. The mission communities that had sustained life in the California outposts when salaries and supplies did not arrive from Mexico were now ordered to be disbanded and transformed to civil use. The changeover was by no means immediate. Priests, appealing to Governor Jose Figueroa, insisted that the Indians in Los Angeles were worse off than the Indians at the missions. There was brutality in the city—white against Indian, white against white—and the neophytes needed protection.

In 1851 Hugo Reid, a Scot who came to settle in 1832, described for the *Los Angeles Star* how San Gabriel was destroyed: "The back buildings were unroofed and the timber converted into firewood. Cattle were killed. . . . Utensils were disposed of, and goods and other articles distributed in profusion among the neophytes. . . . This was a period of demoralization."

Los Angeles was a city with little law and even less order.

(Overleaf) Mock street fight at Universal studio tour; hero Lance Remer knocks out villain Steve Gillam

Pio Pico picks a bride

A marriage in the midst of turbulence: Pio Pico, one of the revolutionaries banished by Governor Victoria at the beginning of the 1830s, came back to marry Maria Ygnacia Alvarado. The celebration was the biggest and grandest ever seen in town, a fiesta lasting eight days and nights. Governor Jose Figueroa was the best man. Fireworks exploded, church bells rang, the entire population of the pueblo came to dance.

The ceremony itself was performed at the Plaza Church. The party moved across the street to the home of the revolutionary leader Jose Antonio Carillo, where the restored Pico House —built as a hotel by Pico in 1869— stands today.

A modern wedding mural, with over-size bride and groom, emblazons a building overlooking the Broadway shopping street where Hispanic residents still come to buy elaborate wedding costumes. Maria Ygnacia Alvarado Pico wore a black silk gown and black lace mantilla for the ceremony, changing into a white dress for the wedding breakfast. She was escorted from the church by a procession of violinists and guitarists.

Mural on the side of a clothing store between Broadway and Spring Street

The little capital that couldn't

Mexico decreed in one of its more comic-opera mandates that the "pueblo of Los Angeles in Alta California is erected into a city, and it will be in the future the capital of that territory." The government in Monterey, the existing capital, was outraged. It maintained that Los Angeles, the little town of saloons, brothels, and gambling houses, was inappropriate and unprepared. Los Angeles had no public buildings worthy of local government, no hotels to accommodate guests of the government, no residence suitable for a governor—and the pueblo was making no effort to erect them.

Los Angeles continued to suffer from mob violence and minor insurrection. The Mexican authorities decided to ignore the new capital and remain at Monterey in civilized surroundings and relative safety.

The Bonaventure Hotel is a symbol of a newly accommodating downtown— developed in the 1960s and 1970s—with its enlarged Civic Center, Music Center, Convention Center, and World Trade Center.

Los Angeles Bonaventure Hotel, offering 1,500 rooms, opened in 1976

93

Violence, vigilance, dirty dogs, and a den of thieves

Life in the unkempt uncapital continued downhill. The local government had to pass a law prohibiting ownership of more than two dogs, because dogs were littering the little city's streets. And by law those animals had to be leashed or tied. Residents were asked to participate in the battle against scavenger birds, which were swooping in to live off the filth.

In 1836 drunken Indians were ordered to help build more water facilities because the supply of fresh water was low. Townsfolk guaranteed a continual force of laborers by feeding liquor to Indians until they were drunk enough to be indentured to the chain gang. An English visitor in Los Angeles described the city at the time as "a den of thieves," with "the lowest drunkards and gamblers of the country."

The first vigilance committee was formed after the body of a local man was found, murdered by his wife's lover. A mob of vigilantes, over the city council's live bodies, stormed the local jail and killed both the assassin-lover and the accomplice wife.

*Dogs at Los Angeles
Animal Shelter*

Further revolting developments

In 1837 Juan Bandini, one of the more consistent revolutionaries of the decade, brought a band of insurgents to Los Angeles and captured the city. This was not the first time an anti-Mexico platoon claimed to have liberated the little pueblo. Los Angeles apparently was not much to liberate, because a few days later Bandini left town for San Diego with only a cache of captured weapons to show for his "revolution."

Local officials came and went, depending upon which crowd of soldiers was commanding the town, those loyal to Mexico or those loyal to revolution. Provisional governor Carlos Antonio Carillo came to power in 1837 as a Mexican appointee and for a time persuaded the people of Los Angeles not to join the movement for an independent California.

But chaos had become habit. Even though Carillo proclaimed Los Angeles as his capital, no one informed Governor Juan Bautista Alvarado in Monterey about any changes. Alvarado and Carillo finally met in Los Angeles to settle the situation peaceably. Alvarado was reconfirmed as governor; Carillo was given the offshore island of Santa Rosa as his reward for relinquishing authority.

(Overleaf) Mexican mural at Lincoln Park; Elaine Alvarado in front of a painting commemorating Bandini's capture of Los Angeles

95

Amid rebellion, small change

Balancing the Los Angeles budget in 1838 was hardly a feat of high finance. As governors came and went, as rebels took the city and then left, as sin and smuggling flourished under the lax local government, Los Angeles closed the year with a budgetary surplus of $3. Expenditures totaled $834; receipts were $837. That amounted to real fiscal responsibility in a city of fewer than 2,000 citizens.

But Los Angeles decided it still could not finance public education. Don Ygnacio Coronel had set up a school in 1836, without much support from the citizenry. For two years he held on, charging about $15 a month for instruction and—for the first time—including young women in the classroom. An earlier governor had opposed educating girls on the grounds that they would learn only to write love letters, thereby distracting the boys as well as themselves. Ironically Coronel's attempt failed during the year of surplus.

Money room in a major Los Angeles bank

Del Valle family granted a rancho, later the setting for Ramona

Grants establishing ranchos continued, even accelerated, during the Mexican period. There was a small land boom following the secularization of the missions. In 1839 Agustin Machado was given La Ballona; Francisco Marquez received Boca de Santa Monica; and Don Antonio del Valle acquired Rancho San Francisco, beautiful hillside country north of San Fernando Valley.

The del Valles already had a home in the Plaza. But that same year Don Antonio was granted a rancho on which his son, Don Ygnacio, later built Camulos, a beautiful ranch house that Helen Hunt Jackson used as the fictional setting for her 1884 novel *Ramona,* one of the earliest tributes to a dying Indian culture.

Every year the First Century Families of Los Angeles gather for a celebration; more than 600 descendants turn out, including the del Valles, who posed for this portrait at the end of one of the festivities. The del Valle house at the Plaza is gone, but Rancho Camulos, under new ownership, has been designated an official California landmark.

Descendants of the early del Valle family at the Fort Moore Pioneer Memorial on Hill Street—from left, Ulpano del Valle II, Antonio Federico del Valle, Nena Marquard Roswell, Paul Marquard Phillips, Ysabel Marquard Phillips, Frances Bermudez Cram, Charles Cram

1840

A smuggler as leading citizen

Abel Stearns was one of the most colorful Americans to settle in Los Angeles. He came from Massachusetts, complete with Harvard education, and in 1840 he was arraigned as a smuggler. At that time people considered smuggling a reasonable occupation even though it was illegal, and the charges against Stearns were dropped because of public pressure. As consolation for the inconvenience of arrest, Stearns was appointed administrator of customs.

At the beginning of the 1830s Stearns had been one of the dissidents banished when Governor Victoria tried to impose one-man rule in California. In the vicinity of the port he owned a warehouse for storing skins; it was conveniently near the coves where contraband was stored. At the age of forty-three Stearns married Maria Francisca Paula Arcadia Bandini, a fourteen-year-old local girl. Called Cara de Caballo—horseface—because of a disfiguring scar, Stearns gave generously to charity so that people would not laugh at the contrast between age and youth, ugliness and beauty, in his marriage. He bought Rancho Los Alamitos and became the largest land and cattle baron in the region. After California became part of the United States, Stearns was elected to the new state legislature. He eventually lost Los Alamitos when he went broke and was unable to pay $152 worth of delinquent taxes.

Labrador retriever sniffs passenger luggage at U.S. Customs at the Port of Los Angeles, trying to smell out contraband from a cruise ship

A mountain to match a man

Benjamin D. Wilson spent fifteen years crossing the plains, trapping and trading, fighting Indians as well as befriending them, after leaving his native Tennessee. In 1841 he joined the Rowland-Workman immigrant party driving sheep from Santa Fe to California.

Like other arriving Americans, Wilson married a local woman, Dona Ramona Yorba of the Santa Ana ranch, assuming Hispanic dignity as Don Benito Wilson. And like many of the American settlers, trader Wilson became rich in Los Angeles. A visitor from Yale later described Wilson as "uneducated, but a man of great force and character," who "is now worth a hundred or more thousand dollars and lives like a prince, only with less luxury."

Wilson became mayor of Los Angeles in 1851 and in 1852 was appointed Indian agent for the region by President Millard Fillmore. Wilson himself described the Indians as "corrupted" after years of "neglect, misrule, oppression, slavery and injustice" during the period following secularization of the missions. He complained about their drinking, but he also deplored their poor wages and extolled their abilities to master crafts.

Mount Wilson, named after Don Benito, stands high above Pasadena, with television transmission towers that serve surrounding communities.

Television antennae on Mount Wilson

Gold without the rush

Don Francisco Lopez left his house on March 8, 1842, to search for stray horses in Placerita Canyon. His wife asked him to look for wild onions while he rode. He noticed some onions below an oak tree beside a stream, and when he dug them up, he observed peculiar golden flecks among the roots. Lopez carefully scraped the flecks off his onions and rode into Los Angeles with them where an assayer confirmed his find. Gold! Prospectors soon trudged into Placerita Canyon to dig and discover. Abel Stearns later accepted a few nuggets as payment for merchandise and shipped them to the U.S. mint in Philadelphia.

This first gold discovery in California was just above San Fernando Valley, and it happened six years before the famous strike up north at Sutter's Mill. But there was no stampede the likes of which trampled Northern California. The total yield at Placerita was worth only about $200,000.

The Oak of the Golden Dream today stands in a county park near a public nature museum.

Young Sandy Lubard marks the spot—the oak tree—where gold was first discovered in California at Placerita Canyon

1843

Invitation to an invader

By 1843 it seemed certain that Mexico would lose its California colony; control and authority were diminishing daily. England, France, and the United States had different but equally selfish designs on the territory, which was clearly up for grabs.

Only the year before, the American commodore Thomas Catesby Jones had conquered the Mexicans at Monterey and raised the U.S. flag over California. But that was a mistake, like so many other premature moves in a war often verging on comic opera. Jones, commander of American naval units in the Pacific, had received a misleading message in 1842 while anchored off Peru. He thought that war had broken out between America and Mexico, and he immediately sailed his fleet to Monterey to prevent any other nation from occupying California. The presidio at Monterey surrendered without a battle. A few days later Jones learned that war was not in progress. With apologies he pulled down the flag and sheepishly sailed back to sea.

In early 1843 Jones was anchored off San Pedro when he received a message from Mexican governor Manuel Micheltorena. Would the commodore meet with the governor to discuss political and military developments? This message was real. Jones went ashore at the port and was surprised to find cooks waiting at the beach to prepare a hot lunch before the American party set off to meet Micheltorena in town. The ensuing conferences were equally polite and full of pomp, promising a peace that could not be maintained.

The U.S.S. Los Angeles, *a nuclear-powered submarine, visits its namesake city*

To arms, to horse, to defend

The original Spanish-speaking residents
of California, known as Californios, had
been fighting with Mexico and with
each other for years. Governors had
come and gone; local insurrections had
risen and fallen; the capital had been
moved from Monterey to Los Angeles
and back again. The Americans had arrived, to marry and to adopt Spanish
names, to become Catholics in many
instances—and to become successful in
a few. Some Americans were welcomed
from the start, but some would always
be suspect.

The year 1844 seemed to be the time
for all good California Mexicans to
come to the aid of Mexico. All able-
bodied men were ordered to join defense
units. The governor appointed Pio Pico
and Jose Antonio Carillo to command
two units of cavalry as the land forces
for Los Angeles. Pico and Carillo were
already famous for waging battle in the
pueblo, both political and personal. Pico
was one of the upstarts banished by
Governor Victoria more than a decade
earlier. Carillo's brother, Don Carlos,
was the man who in 1837 had assumed
the governorship and then later relin-
quished it.

*Long Beach Mounted Police, a
volunteer force performing rescue
missions and parades, exercises
in Rolling Hills*

1845

Insurrection followed by cleanup in high places

The battle of Cahuenga Pass in 1845 was a case of confusion compounded by conflicting loyalties. Former governor Juan Bautista Alvarado was leading an insurrection against Governor Micheltorena. Pio Pico, his brother Andres, and other leading Californios joined Alvarado's revolutionaries. Don Benito Wilson, William Workman, and other leading Americans decided to remain loyal to Micheltorena.

The two forces, which were about equal in number, finally confronted one another at Cahuenga Pass, the slice in the Santa Monica Mountains between Los Angeles and San Fernando Valley. As one early account noted: "The tide of battle raged with varying success throughout that eventful afternoon. Many trees had their limbs broken, and the mountain rabbits were frightened almost to death by the constant explosion of gunpowder."

Don Benito and his troops finally agreed to a truce, promising to recognize Pico as the new governor, and Micheltorena withdrew to Mexico. The Mexican loyalists lost one horse in the carnage; the revolutionaries lost one mule. Although men screamed and women wept, no person had been killed. A cleanup was ordered.

Window washer Richard Tolliver atop Occidental Tower

1846

Los Angeles, capital of California again

War between Mexico and the United States, long delayed, was finally declared in 1846. Mexico made the announcement after General Zachary Taylor established a fort along the Rio Grande on land the Mexicans claimed as their own. This was the same year that two Americans seized the military post at Sonoma and proclaimed the Bear Flag Republic, a California independent from Mexico.

Los Angeles, which under Governor Pio Pico was finally established as the capital of California, prepared to resist the Americans. Pico called for volunteers, but few were still loyal to Mexico. Commodore Robert F. Stockton led a successful expeditionary force into the city, proclaimed California a territory of the United States, and proceeded to organize a government headed by himself.

Victory was as short as it may have been sweet. That same year General Jose Flores retook the city for Mexico, and the Californios held ground for the remainder of the year.

Veterans cemetery in West Los Angeles

Stockton returns and retakes Los Angeles

The battle of La Mesa, in the neighborhood of present Vernon, was Mexico's last stand at Los Angeles. The Americans were advancing across a broad plain between the San Gabriel and Los Angeles rivers. The Californio defenders waited in ambush behind a low hill. General Flores launched a cavalry attack against the invaders; the Americans repelled it, and the war was practically over.

A local peace treaty was signed at an adobe on what is now Lankershim Boulevard, directly across the street

1847

from the starting point of visitors' tours to Universal Studios. The site has been restored. A final peace treaty between Mexico and the United States, the treaty of Guadalupe Hidalgo, was signed later. General Stephen W. Kearny and Commodore Stockton were trying to unravel conflicting orders as to which man would govern American California. Confusion returned. But the Americans were coming, and they continue to come by plane, car, and jogging shoe.

(Overleaf) The Brentwood marathon, 6.2 miles of modern American stamina

1848

*Los Angeles becomes
part of the United States*

American takeover of California was by design not dramatic. President James Polk's peace proclamation of July 1848 spared the life of a Los Angeles Mexican charged with bearing arms after the Americans had won the city. The ayuntamiento, or town council, was restored just after the U.S. occupation. American policy was to preserve what order remained and not disturb those institutions that were capable of functioning.

But changes were coming. Many Protestants would be arriving to take up residence in what had been a Catholic city. Capitalists, who saw land as a resource for selling rather than for granting, were also coming. The period of rapid expansion in Los Angeles under the Americans began the same year that James Wilson Marshall discovered gold in the north, turning quiet California the following year into a carnival of prospectors.

The First Congregational Church was built in the early 1930s; the 1972 CNA Building, mirroring the church and changing times, was designed by the architectural firm of Langdon & Wilson.

First Congregational Church reflected in the glass modernity of the CNA Building at Lafayette Park

First real survey of a city

War was expensive. Los Angeles, like most of California, was broke. The Americans decided to sell public land to build up the public treasures.

But nobody knew where to establish proper boundaries. No specific city map existed. Lieutenant Edward O. C. Ord, stationed in Monterey, had some knowledge of surveying. He would delineate Los Angeles, he said, for payment and a piece of property amounting to 160 acres. No property, declared the government. Ord then agreed to do the work for cash on the line—$3,000.

The city in 1849 was bounded by Pico Boulevard on the south, Figueroa—then called Calle de las Chapules (street of grasshoppers)—on the west, Los Angeles River on the east, and San Fernando Road on the north. Ord brought in his survey by November; more than fifty lots were immediately put up for sale and purchased for between $50 and $200. Land speculation in Los Angeles had started.

Land surveyor Pete Messano sights on the new $42 million sewage treatment facility for Terminal Island

California becomes the thirty-first state

California was admitted into the Union in September 1850, following strong arguments over whether the former Mexican colony should be a territory or a full-fledged state.

Los Angeles had sent delegates to a convention in Monterey, which culminated in a state constitution signed in 1849. At the time of California's admission, Los Angeles was proclaimed a self-governing city within Los Angeles County, a sprawling area almost as large as the state of Ohio. The new county included all of present Orange and San Bernardino counties and parts of Kern and Riverside counties. Americans, not Californios, held most of the high offices; Dr. Alpheus P. Hodges, a Virginian with real estate interests in town, was elected mayor.

Large as the county was, important as the city was, Los Angeles at the time of California statehood lacked a functioning public school, an established newspaper, and even a proper bank—merchants kept their cash along with valuables in small iron safes in their stores.

(Overleaf) Los Angeles, largest city in the state of California, at night

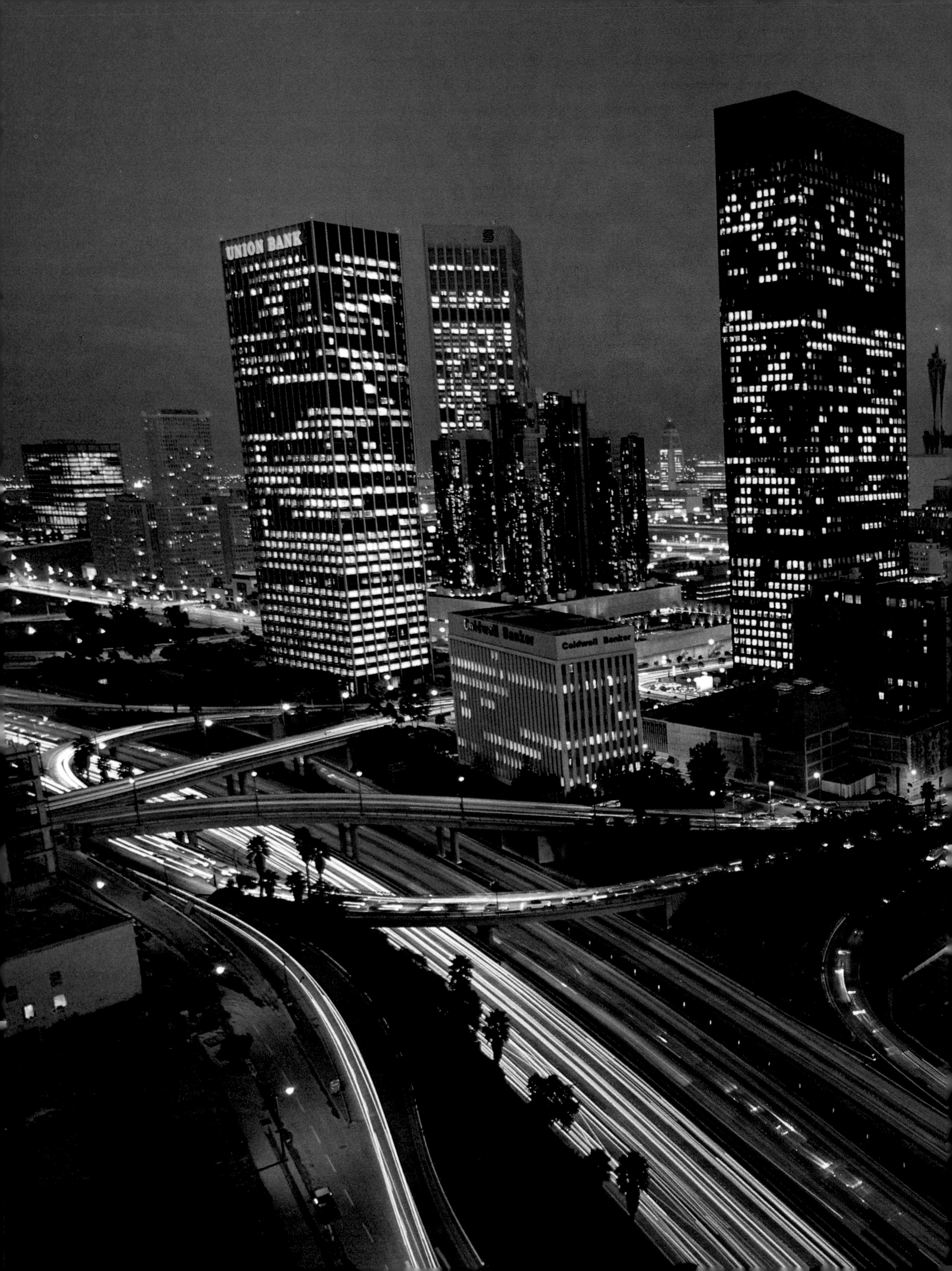
UNION BANK
Coldwell Banker

A born-again boomtown

The 1850s was a decade of firsts for the City of the Angels:

John Gregg Nichols was the first Anglo child born in the city.

The *Star*, Los Angeles's first newspaper, began publishing in English and Spanish, thus forming a basis for bilingualism in a city still struggling with bilingual arguments.

The first real police force was organized.

The first wooden house was built.

The first stagecoach line was created by Phineas Banning.

The first meeting of Masons was held.

And the first group of Mormons arrived from Salt Lake City; 437 men, women, and children came in 150 ox-drawn wagons.

Babyland, a section of Forest Lawn Memorial Park

Land battles and brick buildings

The new building of the city brick by brick began in 1852. Brick replaced adobe, making multistoried construction feasible for the first time. In 1852 Captain Jesse D. Hunter opened the first kiln, and the first brick house was finished the following year at the corner of Third and Main. Within the decade brick became big business; the firm of Mullaly, Porter & Ayers sold two million building blocks in 1858 alone.

But there were major controversies at ground level. The U.S. Congress was challenging Spanish and Mexican land grants, demanding proof of private ownership and denying all grants made after American annexation in 1846. In some cases, records had been lost; in others, landmarks for boundaries had disappeared as a result of drought, fire, or flood. As the federal land commission held hearings, rancho owners lost ground—because of legal costs, lack of records, or uncertainty. The days of the rancho were ending; 40 percent of the legitimate land grants wound up being auctioned or lost to litigation or creditors.

Brick residential structure on Sixth Street, Skid Row

Other Christians are coming

The Reverend Adam Bland bought a saloon in 1853 and converted it into Los Angeles's first Methodist church. A Presbyterian, James Wood, arrived in the city the same year, hoping to begin regular services. But a congregation did not form around him, and Wood left town. A Reverend Freeman organized the first Baptist assembly in town. And the Mormon community of San Bernardino became a county in its own name, carved out of land previously assigned to Los Angeles.

The growing piety among residents had not ended an Indian slave market in downtown Los Angeles. American vineyard owners paid Indian workers with aguardiente—"a veritable fire water," according to writer and ranger Horace Bell. With plenty of booze but no money the Indians naturally spent the weekend drinking downtown. Then on Sunday at sundown the local marshal rounded them up and herded them into a guarded corral, where they would sleep off their binges to be available for sale on Monday morning to the next vineyard bidder. The cycle was indeed vicious: work through Saturday; payoff in aguardiente; drunk Saturday night and Sunday; sobering up Sunday night; sale on Monday; work through Saturday; a new payday in drink. Back-breaking toil, debilitating drink, a short-lived future of squalor and poverty—such was the "salvation" the missionaries had promised.

(Overleaf) An international convention of Jehovah's Witnesses assembles at Dodger Stadium

119

1854

*A rickety road and a fort
that defended against rustling*

Fort Tejon helped in the struggle against cattle rustling in the hills around Tejon Pass. It was also a place where troops or travelers could rest on their way through the rugged San Gabriel Mountains. In 1854 travel was still tough going. The Los Angeles County Supervisors finally voted $1,000 to build a wagon road linking San Fernando Mission with the western portions of San Fernando Valley. "A rather broad trail already existed there," wrote merchant Harris Newmark in his classic study of Los Angeles life, *Sixty Years in Southern Cailfornia,* "but such was its grade that many a pioneer, compelled to use a windlass or other con-

trivance to let down his wagon in safety, will never forget the real perils of the descent. For years it was a familiar experience with stages, on which I sometimes traveled, to attach chains or boards to retard their downward movement; nor were passengers even then without anxiety until the hill or mountainside had been passed."

In the same neighborhood Americans today choose to ride a roller coaster called Colossus for a price, the peril of one century having become the pleasure park of another.

Colossus, world's largest roller coaster, at Magic Mountain near Tejon Pass

1855

School comes back to town

Education enjoyed its own roller coaster history in Los Angeles; schools opened and closed depending on the rise and fall of enthusiasm. A major effort to teach the citizens began in 1855 with a real schoolhouse at the corner of Spring and Second.

The *Star* noted a discrepancy: "There are now 1,191 children between the ages of four and eighteen in Los Angeles, El Monte, and San Gabriel school districts; yet not more than 150 in all attend school." A new superintendent was elected, and the mayor pushed for new educational laws. But the citizens were still more interested in raising cattle than in rearing educated youngsters. Schools received few public funds and roused little public ardor until 1860, when the state finally began appropriating money for education—nearly $2,500 for Los Angeles County.

The first-grade class with teacher Claudia Lee at Rosemont Elementary School near downtown

1856

Beer garden concerts, crime, and cattle losses

The year 1856 was not a propitious one. The cattle business was about bust. A drought had parched the grazing lands, causing the deaths of 100,000 cattle by starvation. Ranch owners, already hurting from the land grant litigations, could not afford to improve their breeds. The relationships between the Californios and the Anglos had also been strained by land-ownership controversies, sometimes marked by racial violence.

The city was full of saloons, prostitutes, bandits, and vigilantes. Yet culture, like schooling, was slowly being introduced. A French sailor named Ramon Alexander landed in Los Angeles and built a beer garden called the Round House. Along with the brews, he provided open-air concerts for the citizenry.

The Arco garage concerts, sponsored by Atlantic Richfield, Bank of America, and the American Federation of Musicians Trust Fund, were started in the 1970s. The performances feature folk music, pop, and jazz, attracting crowds who sit in the sunshine, eat brown-bag lunches, and enjoy the programs.

Free summer lunchtime concerts atop Arco garage

1857

Precious water in a pipeline

The city authorized its first pipeline system in 1857, three years after Water Resources became an official department within local government. By 1860 the first real waterworks were in operation. A waterwheel at the mother ditch near College and Alameda streets fed water from the river to a brick reservoir at the Plaza. The original pipes were simple hollow logs.

Nature had its own schedule that year, beginning with a violent earthquake in January, followed by snow and then by rainstorms in spring and by thunderstorms in December. More water reportedly fell during a period of thirty-six hours at the end of the year than had fallen in the previous three years. The dread of drought was suddenly replaced by the terror of washout.

Violence was prevalent along with the storms. Members of the Juan Flores gang, terrorists and guerrilla warriors, were captured and jailed. But vigilantes rode ahead of justice and hanged eleven members of the gang before a trial was held.

Marvin Floyd monitors the storage area at Ameron Pipe Company in South Gate

Butterfield, the next stage of development

John Butterfield was hired to follow in Phineas Banning's stagecoach tracks. Banning had been the trailblazer between San Fernando Valley and Northern California, not only building stage lines from the harbor to Los Angeles but also opening a route through San Fernando Pass to stimulate trade with the communities to the north. Local merchants were to help finance the stage line, but they balked at the steep grades as well as steep costs. Banning himself had arranged a stagecoach demonstration to prove the practicability of his plan by driving down the pass while would-be contributors watched on foot. The project went ahead, the work being accomplished by Chinese labor.

Within one year a train of mule teams plied the ground between Los Angeles and Fort Tejon, a distance of seventy-five miles that took nine days of travel.

The federal government hired Butterfield to begin mail service by coach in 1858. Armed guards protected passengers and posted letters along a route connecting Saint Louis, El Paso, Los Angeles, and San Francisco. Butterfield later put his experience to good use in private enterprise and organized American Express.

The Butterfield Stage—complete with Hollywood holdup man—recreated at Knott's Berry Farm, an Orange County amusement park

A distant mirror of a market

Now that Los Angeles had routes connecting it to the outside world, trade was becoming organized. There was a newspaper, a post office, the beginnings of a telegraph line, and the Bella Union Hotel. The first city market opened in 1859, the same year the Protestant ministers decided to establish a combined church.

Yet business remained somewhat casual. Harris Newmark's *Reminiscences* included colorful comments on the merchants and market men of his day: "Proprietors would sometimes close their stores and go out for an hour or two for their meals, or to meet in a friendly game of billiards. During the monotonous days when but little business was being transacted, it was not uncommon for merchants to visit back and forth and to spend hours at a time playing cards."

The shopping area itself was equally unorganized. No real sidewalks existed downtown; thus pedestrians dragged through the dust during dry months and slogged through the mud during the rainy seasons. Abel Stearns, the onetime smuggler, continued to prosper. He had built his Arcadia block in Los Angeles in 1858 and his various properties had been assessed at $186,000. Thus a crucial question: Were sidewalks really necessary?

Escalator at Bullock's in the Northridge Shopping Center in San Fernando Valley

The ooze makes news

Merchant Jonathan Temple tried to improve the street scene by paving his block along Main with bricks and then covering them smoothly with asphalt made from the ooze at Rancho La Brea. But with summer's heat the asphalt turned to ooze again, and pedestrians began sticking in it like the prehistoric beasts trapped centuries earlier.

Explorer Gaspar de Portola had noticed the peculiar tar pools at La Brea as early as 1769. The Los Angeles pioneers brought the tar into town to use as a waterproof roof covering. It was effective until the following summer, when the ooze melted off the tops of houses and ran down the adobe walls.

Scientific exploration of the pits was begun in 1906 by the University of California, which turned up a zoo full of prehistoric animal skeletons preserved in the tar. Exploration has continued, by funding fits and paleontologic starts, ever since. Today the Page Museum, part of the County Museum of Natural History, is located near the tar pits.

La Brea tar pits at Hancock Park, where prehistoric animals were trapped during the Ice Age

Rains and river rampage

The rains began on Christmas Eve and nearly drowned the town. Adobe buildings collapsed from the weight of water; vineyards and gardens were flushed out of the ground and carried into the river. Before the heavens ran dry early in 1862, as much as fifty inches of rain had fallen on Los Angeles in less than a month, more than three times the normal annual rainfall.

Cattle died, business stopped, no mail was delivered to the city. The only contact with the outside world came by steamer at the harbor in San Pedro. Early in 1861 the schooner *Lewis Perry* had sailed into San Pedro carrying freight—it was the first such vessel towed across the sandbar and tied to a new wharf. Converting the harbor into a cargo port for Los Angeles seemed to make sense.

The present-day parade of boats at Christmastime is a light show in the harbor, with prizes awarded to those owners who make their vessels resemble decorated trees at sea.

(Overleaf) Christmas afloat, annual parade of lighted boats at Los Angeles Harbor

1862

Camels walked for miles carrying Civil War supplies

By 1862 camels had been carrying supplies across the Mojave Desert for about five years. Beasts that had begun life in Arabia were sent all the way to Texas and then strapped with 600 pounds of cargo. They trekked to Fort Tejon above San Fernando Valley and then meandered through downtown Los Angeles in an exotic caravan, lines of camels plodding straight through the city.

After Fort Tejon was inactivated by the federal government, the camels were housed in a Main Street corral between First and Second streets to await assignments. The animals' dislike of city life was vented on gaping citizens, who were kicked at and sometimes even bitten. Camel caravans were transferred to Drum Barracks at San Pedro and were pressed into government service during the Civil War. The animals were eventually consigned to civilian use as freight carriers in Nevada and Arizona, and some were simply set free in the desert—mirages of Araby on American plains.

The Los Angeles Zoo, built in the 1960s, at Griffith Park

1863

From drenched to dry again

Southern Californians knew there was a Civil War on far away, between states north and states south, but they had more immediate troubles of their own. As Robert Glass Cleland later wrote in *The Cattle on a Thousand Hills,* "The great flood of 1861–62 was followed by two years of unparalleled drought. Almost no rain fell during the ensuing fall or winter; and by spring [1863], cattle on many of the southern ranges were in desperate straits." Cleland also described the "hard, scorching winds from the desert," sweeping millions of grasshoppers "across the country like a devastating fire."

Worse still was the epidemic of smallpox. The whole region was ravaged, but the Mexican and Indian populations were especially afflicted. Deaths in the pueblo were so numerous that the municipal authorities discontinued tolling of the church bells. Vaccine was scarce, available only by steamer from San Francisco, and there were few doctors. Rancher Don Juan Forster, later in a legal proceeding, bitterly depicted the seasons of 1863 and 1864 as "a perfect devastation."

Bottoms up in a drought-proof swimming hole

1864

Banning builds his dream house

Phineas Banning was still enjoying a profitable time; the man who had established a stage line between the port and Los Angeles finished his home in Wilmington near the harbor. But 1864 was another poor year for most of his fellow citizens. H. D. Barrows wrote from Los Angeles to the San Francisco *Bulletin:* "Except one rain, about the middle of last November, we have had no rain of consequence for nearly a year, nor enough to make a good crop of grass for nearly two years. . . . Thousands and thousands of cattle have died, and are dying, and those that are left. . . stalk about like spectres. The heavens are as brass; the clouds all blow away and bring no rain." There were a few showers in February, followed first by nasty sandstorms and then by unseasonable heat in May and scorching heat in summer. Not until November did the calamitous heat cool under heavy rains.

Meanwhile, Phineas Banning was using his new home as a rallying place for Union forces during the Civil War. The restored house is now a museum with tours sponsored by the Los Angeles City Department of Recreation and Parks.

General Phineas Banning Residence in Wilmington

1865

*A public park from
lack of private interest*

Ugly land lay idle just west of the city. Nothing grew on the soil, which was permeated with alkali. During rare but heavy rains, the bare earth became a swamp of mud.

At public auction in 1865 the swamp was put up for sale at the price of twenty-five cents an acre, which was modest even at the going rates. Yet there were no offers. The land remained a muddy eyesore for two more decades, until Mayor William Workman decided to do something green about it. With public greenbacks and private donations he added topsoil and trees, carved a lake out of a natural depression, and proclaimed the place Westlake Park (later renamed MacArthur Park, after the World War II general).

Today it is a refuge for ducks and drunks and elderly neighbors, who play out their afternoons at public game boards.

Pawn to pleasure at MacArthur Park

1866

New people, prosperity, and poker playing

The American Civil War was over; throngs of people were moving west, seeking new opportunities and the prosperity that was, according to one local journalist, permanent.

Immigration was welcome, but not all the newcomers were assets. As philanthropist Dr. J. P. Widney pessimistically noted: "Men of questionable character, men of no character, drifted in. Money was plentiful, and the gamblers found a congenial field." Gambling was one of the earliest pastimes in Los Angeles, brought there by the trappers, Chinese laborers, and prospectors who drifted down after the Gold Rush.

Whether gambling is mild vice or serious sin is a continual argument in Southern California. Gambling could be found wherever there was chance—at racetracks, poker parlors (legal in Gardena), and the nearby gaming tables of Nevada. Bingo, an innocuous social diversion, was not approved in Los Angeles until the 1970s, when almost immediately it became an attraction for charities, churches, synagogues, and senior-citizen centers.

Legal bingo at Temple Beth Ami in San Fernando Valley

1867

A light unto the streets

Until 1867 nightfall meant dark and dangerous streets in Los Angeles. As merchant Harris Newmark described it: "In those nights of dark streets and still darker tragedies, people rarely went out unless equipped with candle-burning lanterns." But improvements came with prosperity. W. H. Perry won a franchise to bring gaslight into Los Angeles.

Perry's program was a limited one. For the next five years, until electricity was authorized, there were only 136 gas lamps serving a city of 12,000 people. The first twenty-five lamps burned gas made from local tar and imported coal. The mayor's office and Main Street were illuminated free of charge.

Even with lighted streets fear of crime was real in those days. The city council passed a law the same year prohibiting all citizens—except law officers and travelers—from carrying guns, knives, swords, or even slingshots. The law was not enforced because the public refused to give up its arms.

Blue gas flame, produced by electricity, above Southern California Gas Company headquarters—employee Gerri Mannon standing by

At last a city to bank on

The banking business in Los Angeles was begun in 1868. Not one, but two banks opened. Hayward & Company was a partnership between John Hayward of San Francisco and former governor John Downey. Hellman, Temple & Company was a combine of local merchants. The Hayward firm started out with $100,000 capital; the Hellmans had $25,000 more.

Before banks were introduced, Los Angeles merchants kept iron safes in their shops in which established customers could deposit money, without interest, for safekeeping. Residents generally hid their money at home. Travelers often were robbed because they had no suitable hiding places for their cash.

Bundles of bills stacked in a present-day Los Angeles financial institution

Tracks to the harbor

Senator Phineas Banning, Los Angeles's prime mover, had been pushing for a railroad between port and city for years. As early as 1861 the state authorized local government to raise funds, and by 1864 citizens were arguing the how and where of such a line. In 1868 the city and county managed to persuade the electorate to pass a bond issue.

As rapidly as October the following year the twenty-one-mile railroad was finished and ready for opening-day excursions. The *Los Angeles News* reported the ride as follows: "Two trains . . . were run . . . and both were crowded to their utmost capacity; not less than 1,500 people made the round trip. The heat and dust detracted somewhat from the enjoyment of the occasion; but in the main it was heartily enjoyed."

In the same year that Los Angeles built its track to San Pedro the Transcontinental Railroad, tying California to the rest of the country, was completed when the golden spike joining the western and eastern sections of track was hammered down in Utah.

Looking north toward City Hall along the old rail line

A first-class hotel, for a change

The Pico brothers, Andres and ex-governor Pio, wanted to bring respectability and luxury back to the Plaza. They bought the old Carillo home and proceeded to build a fancy hotel, the best in Southern California. Pico House was the first three-storied structure in town, and it boasted the added attraction of a bathroom on every floor. There was a central patio at street level, gas lighting, a glorious ballroom, and even a big-name chef.

Inspired by the Picos, William Abbott built the Merced Theater next door. Los Angeles now had legitimate drama and luxury at the same time. But the Plaza could not live up to its new dignity. It had already become a place of recurrent violence and vandalism. Old residents were moving out, abandoning their town houses for their ranchos.

Pico House has been restored as the centerpiece of a designated state historical park at the Plaza. The Merced remains standing next door. The New Otani, a luxury hotel opened in 1978 in Little Tokyo, is part of a redevelopment area that seems to be successful, with new churches and shopping malls as well as new housing for elderly residents.

The New Otani Hotel with Japanese garden atop its parking garage; Saint Vibiana's Cathedral, built in the 1870s, is in the background

A monstrous madness toward Chinese

By 1871 there were only 175 Chinese living in Los Angeles. They had moved south after the Gold Rush subsided and the railroad was finished, and they became cheap local labor, in many cases doing the household chores previously performed by blacks or Indians. The Chinese opened laundries, sold foodstuffs, dug ditches. Many of them were crowded into the huts of the Calle de los Negros, a collection of dilapidated adobes below the Plaza.

The larger community treated the Chinese with indifference or antagonism. Then in 1871 the tensions exploded in what one historian has called "the single most monstrous act of racial hatred in California history." An internecine bloodletting had begun between two rival Chinese tongs. A police officer tried to stop the shooting but suffered a bullet wound for his efforts. When rancher Robert Thompson came to the policeman's rescue, he was fatally shot in the cross fire. A white mob formed, swelled, and spilled over blockades set up by police and sheriffs. More than 400 rioters began looting and lynching. When it was all over, nineteen Chinese had been hanged.

A grand jury indicted nearly fifty rioters after the lynchings. A later trial convicted only a handful of them as murderers or accessories to murder. But subsequently all convictions were overturned on appeal.

Today Chinatown is a neighborhood of relative peace, where tea cakes are served in good restaurants, trinkets are offered in tourist shops, and clothes are sewn—unbeknown to visitors—in latterday sweatshops.

(Overleaf) New Chinatown, tourist attraction with tea cakes

1872

*A library lights up
a once-illiterate city*

As 1872 approached, Los Angeles still lacked a public library. But that year four small dark rooms were set aside in the old Downey Block at Spring Street and Temple. Here a library was established, initially funded by citizen subscription.

Literacy and library interest grew, and by the 1920s the need for a major downtown facility became apparent. Bertram Goodhue and Carleton Winslow were hired to design a building that would become a landmark as well as a continuing controversy. Goodhue and Winslow borrowed and then bedazzled by creating a structure like no other in town. The 1926 library is an incredible amalgam of international influences—Egyptian, Roman, Byzantine, Mediterranean, Islamic.

By the 1960s Los Angeles had outgrown its beloved library, the nation's largest circulating system. But plans and proposals for a new central library came and went like equally needed transit schemes. The new-old library remains the town's central bookshelf, a focus of local pride surrounded by high-rising monuments to oil and finance.

The Los Angeles Public Library, a 1926 low-rise below the towers of Arco and Bank of America

1873

*A colony becomes
Crown of the Valley*

The San Gabriel Valley was orange-growing country in 1873. When the San Gabriel Orange Grove Association bought 4,000 acres of land in that year, a group called the California Colony of Indiana (founded in Indianapolis) was already occupying part of the territory. Also in 1873 subdivision and development were begun by the Orange Grove Association; two years later the members were asked to choose a name for their new city: Indianola, Granada, or Pasadena. The name Pasadena, meaning valley, derives from Chippewa; modern translators like to add another Chippewa word, *weoquan,* to make the city Crown of the Valley. Pasadena was the crowning choice.

Pasadena became the center of the land boom of the 1880s, a major community in its own right, a city that would sustain growth, culture, conservatism, redevelopment, and smog right alongside Los Angeles.

(Overleaf) Pasadena's civic center, a 1920s slice of Spain

A new light on the Pacific

Point Fermin Lighthouse, a shining symbol of new prosperity and a beacon of safe trade, was built in 1874 on a bluff above the harbor. Situated next to a residential neighborhood in San Pedro, the four-sided and slatted lighthouse looks more like a home than a navigational aid.

Farming was doing well the year that the light went on. Export farm goods amounted to more than 48 million pounds; more than 350 steamers and nearly 100 sailing vessels plied in and out of Los Angeles's port. Civil serenity had also become a goal. Los Angeles outlawed prostitution, and, perhaps a more radical move, a law requiring saloon licenses was passed. Before the year was out, Tiburcio Vasquez, prince of the bandits, was peaceably captured and faced a legal trial rather than a summary lynching.

Point Fermin Lighthouse

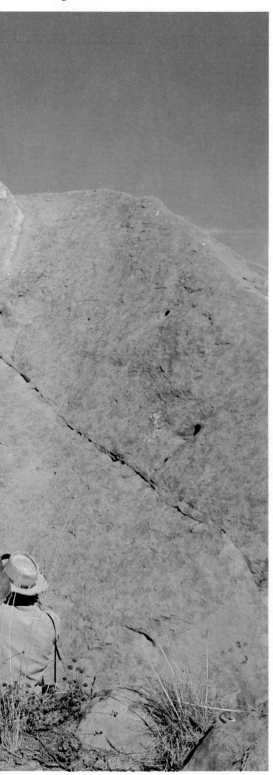

1875

*From fugitive hideout
to fame in the flicks*

Tiburcio Vasquez became the most famous bandit of Los Angeles. Rampaging murderer to some, Mexican Robin Hood to others, Vasquez came down from Monterey to lead a band of desperadoes, to rob stagecoaches, raid outposts, and kidnap citizens for ransom.

His favorite hideout was among the jagged rocks of Soledad Canyon north of the town. The ranchers in the vicinity felt terrorized, but romantics spoke about the mysterious Mexican who rode around avenging injustice perpetrated by the Americans. The governor was so angered by Vasquez's success that he offered an $8,000 reward to anyone who could bring in the bandit alive.

Vasquez was taken in 1874 while visiting his friend Greek George in West Hollywood. Vasquez leaped out of a window to escape the posse dispatched by Sheriff Billy Rowland. A lawman wounded him before he reached his horse, and he was later brought to trial in San Jose. The verdict was guilty and the sentence, carried out in March 1875, was death by hanging.

The jagged rocks favored by the bandit are now known as Vasquez Rocks. They are used for present-day hideouts as well as for gunfight scenes and supernatural backdrops in motion pictures and television.

Vasquez Rocks, an outcrop of earth and sandstone, now a frequent setting for motion pictures

1876

Los Angeles linked to San Francisco via Soledad Canyon

When the United States celebrated its first 100 years, the once-remote city of Los Angeles was finally tied by railroad tracks to the splendid city of San Francisco as well as to the rest of the country. To mark the tie-up between San Francisco and Los Angeles a golden spike was driven at Soledad Canyon near Newhall, and Los Angeles celebrated with a banquet and other festivities. But animosity flared up when Los Angeles discovered that San Francisco paid less for the same rail service between the two towns. When railroad director Charles Crocker came south to address a Los Angeles council meeting, he became so irritated by the southerners that he warned he would make "grass grow in the streets of your city."

Los Angeles celebrated the national centennial with an enormous parade, which was recorded by J. J. Warner, Benjamin Hayes, and J. P. Widney in a centennial history: "There were crowds of people coming into the city by car and carriage, buggy and wagon. They were coming on horseback and afoot, and they continued to come. They came by train from all parts of the county: Tustin City, Richland, Anaheim, Wilmington, Santa Monica, San Fernando. . . . There never was such a crowd in the city before. With one or two exceptions, everybody was on good behavior." Some 1,500 spectators watched from seats placed along the line of march, while official Orator of the Day John Eastman made his pronouncement to the City of Angels that America would become "queen of the earth."

Train on the historic tracks through Soledad Canyon

1877

Prudent Beaudry prepares for dry years

Prudent Beaudry, a French-Canadian, was one of the local leaders determined to keep the Los Angeles basin in water. In 1877 he built the Angeleno Heights reservoir, which promptly became known as Beaudry's, a name that lives on as the watering place and restaurant in the Bonaventure Hotel.

Beaudry was one of the original water distributors. He was also one of the first downtown subdividers and one of the civic leaders who pushed for cleaning up an old campground now called Pershing Square. In 1872 Beaudry won city permission to lay pipes up Bunker Hill and pump private well water up to his new development.

Water storage in the Hollywood reservoir began in 1924, a year after the Department of Water and Power built its first concrete gravity-type dam.

Lake Hollywood, a reservoir near Cahuenga Pass

1878

A boom in brides and grooms

It was a time to pledge and to promise. In 1878, only sixteen years after municipal marriage practices became local law, Los Angeles saw 2,720 couples come together. Divorce, while possible, was hardly popular; only 122 couples came apart during the same year.

Those were green growing times. A pavilion for agricultural exhibits opened on Temple Street in the same year. A group of bachelors, perhaps anticipating their own destinies, sponsored a "baby show" in the pavilion.

The Bel-Air Hotel has become one of the most popular marriage grounds in Los Angeles. On weekends weddings occur at least once a day, and on some days even more frequently. Judge David Aisenson presides in the garden, a place where pairs of swans paddle by, sycamores create natural canopies, and modern couples embark on matrimony on the banks of residential luxury.

Wedding at the Bel-Air Hotel featuring Dona Trafficanda of Canoga Park and Steven Silkey of Encino

1879

A wharf for Santa Monica

Santa Monica, which was cradled in a great curve of the ocean, protected by offshore islands, and nuzzled by nearby mountains, had important ambitions of its own. Senator John Jones of Nevada had developed the community with commerce in mind, including a railroad, a port, and a resort for the rich. Southern Pacific took over the railroad tracks in 1877, tore down an old wharf in 1878, and tried later to establish Santa Monica as a major port for Los Angeles to rival San Pedro.

In 1879 several local leaders formed the South Santa Monica Wharf and Shipping Company to build a new wharf with warehouses and to grade a wagon road from the wharf to downtown Los Angeles. The ground was now prepared for the great harbor-selection battle to follow, involving not only San Pedro and Santa Monica but also Redondo, the nearby beach community where Captain John Ainsworth of Portland had built a wharf with railroad connection to Los Angeles.

Santa Monica already had a hotel and bathhouse, two churches, a school, and 350 permanent residents. In its advertisements the Santa Monica Hotel boasted about its favorable climate—"the least variable of that of any point in the United States, if not the world." The community was ready to realize its ambitions.

Vanessa Jones walks between the pilings under Santa Monica Pier

For higher education, fight on

The first college that opened in Los Angeles was Saint Vincent's (now Loyola-Marymount University), a Catholic institution established in 1865. Helping the Vincentian fathers was Mrs. Rose Newmark, a Jew who organized a fund-raising fair.

The first Protestant school of higher education was the University of Southern California, chartered in 1880. Ozro Childs, a Protestant, donated 308 lots to raise construction money; former governor John Downey, a Roman Catholic, also pitched in; so did the Jewish businessman Isaias Hellman. Ecumenical contributions continued to arrive in the same spirit that once had aided the opening of Saint Vincent's. Dr. Joseph P. Widney, brother of a major donor, left his medical practice to become the university's first president; he personally guaranteed payment of the school's debts within four years. Right after USC came Occidental College, Pomona College, Redlands, Whittier, and a new local branch of the state normal school.

USC, which ended its Methodist ties in 1929, today enjoys a high academic standing, having schools of law, medicine, dentistry, architecture, and music, among others. USC is also known for sports, winning Rose Bowl football games and singing "Fight On," the battle song of the Los Angeles Trojans.

University of Southern California graduation

Centennial for a city

In 1881 Elias Jackson Baldwin built a cottage in the style of Queen Anne, a place where he could entertain his friends. Lucky Baldwin, as he was known to those friends, was one of the West's great moneymen. Investor, silver speculator, land developer, and racehorse baron, Baldwin was often called the patriarch of Santa Anita. Baldwin was so wealthy later in the decade he was able to lend money to bankers when a land boom went bust.

Los Angeles celebrated its 100th birthday in September 1881 with a great parade and speeches in English, Spanish, and French, congratulating a town that had swelled to more than 11,000 residents. Optimism was already a catchword for opportunism. People were poised for the new rise in land values just around the turn of the calendar.

Baldwin's cottage is now part of the grounds of the Los Angeles State and County Arboretum, a California historical landmark across the street from Baldwin's beloved racetrack.

Jean Atkinson of Pasadena and Bonnie Golden of El Monte celebrate 100 years of Los Angeles at Baldwin Cottage

161

1882

Electrical power to the people

By 1882 Los Angeles businessmen were pressuring for better street lighting. The *Los Angeles Times,* a new newspaper in town, began its second year of publication by joining the campaign "to light the city by electricity." In December 150-foot masts carrying three arc lamps apiece were in place downtown. When Mayor J. R. Toberman threw the magic switch, the city "burst into brilliance," wrote Omar W. Holden in a later history of local power.

Attorney Eddy Feldman's 1972 history *The Art of Street Lighting in Los Angeles* cites the original electrical contract as a promise that "all of the streets and sidewalks . . . now lighted by gas shall be lighted up equally as well if not better by said electric lights . . . and all of said space shall be as light if not lighter than now lighted."

The same year electric lights went on downtown, the telephone was introduced to Los Angeles. Technology was changing communications lines along with sight lines.

Streetlight in San Gabriel, seen through the branches of a crape myrtle tree

The business of big business

Businessmen could feel a coming boom in their bones. The Los Angeles Board of Trade was established in 1883. J. W. Robinson opened a new store at the corner of Spring and Temple; he called it Boston Dry Goods, and from these modest beginnings later developed a chain of stores carrying Robinson's own name.

In the early 1880s Southern Pacific was laying more rails, nailing down the tracks to Yuma, Arizona, connecting them with the Texas Pacific, tying Los Angeles by direct trains to the East. Tracks made trade; trains meant transcontinental exchange.

The Pacific Design Center was built, appropriately enough, on Southern Pacific land in 1975—a giant attempt to put the interiors trades under one massive blue roof. Both critics and admirers immediately called Cesar Pelli's architecture for Victor Gruen Associates "the blue whale." The exterior of the building does dominate its neighborhood at San Vicente Boulevard. The interior celebrates modern geometry—and, gee-whiz, another local success story.

Pacific Design Center, a monumental interior to interiors merchandising

1884

Eccentricity arrives on foot

Los Angeles was ripe for the unconventional arrival of Charles Fletcher Lummis in 1884. Harrison Gray Otis had agreed to pay Lummis's expenses for walking cross-country from Ohio to Los Angeles, if Lummis would write newspaper stories on the way.

He came by himself, covering 3,507 side-tripping miles in 143 days, fighting off wildcats, bandits, and mosquitoes. And he came to stay, first as city editor of the *Los Angeles Times,* later as city librarian, magazine publisher, museum founder, champion of Indian rights, preserver of mission architecture, homebuilder, and general gadfly. Lummis made noises and made good, a latter-day pioneer who brought culture and scholarship to the community along with his personal ambition.

His hand-built stone home, El Alisal (place of the sycamores), still stands near the Pasadena Freeway, not far from the Southwest Museum he helped found to celebrate Indian history. Lummis died in 1928, long before freeways, before walkers eased their way by thumb, before the rest of the United States developed an envy of the eccentricities that settled so naturally in Southern California.

Modern hitchhiker, backpacked and bearded for the road

1885

Only in Los Angeles— a socialist subdivider

H. Gaylord Wilshire was no less unusual than Charles Lummis. In 1885 he subdivided a tract between Sixth and Seventh streets just west of downtown and paved a wide roadway down the center—Wilshire Boulevard. Wilshire was also interested in fields other than land speculation. He became a champion of free public speaking, inviting his own arrest by flouting a local law against using public parks for political speeches. He started a Socialist newspaper, *The Weekly Nationalist,* and ran for Congress. Although he was not elected, Wilshire piled up more votes than any other Socialist in the country at that time.

Wilshire was also rich—from land and a billboard monopoly as well as from a large inheritance, an advantageous marriage, and sound investments. He made fortunes, spent fortunes, lost fortunes. His boulevard would become a great route of capitalist commerce that would eventually run from downtown westward, through the wealth of Beverly Hills, farther on to the new high-rises of Westwood, through the affluence of Brentwood, and at last to the bluffs above the ocean at Santa Monica.

Parade of Masks up Wilshire Boulevard, sponsored by Los Angeles Craft and Folk Art Museum

1886

Road to riches is cheapest by rail

A railroad rate war was on in 1886. The Atchison, Topeka & Santa Fe was in frenzied competition with the Southern Pacific to determine which great line could carry the most people to California. Prosperity was arriving by railroad coach. On one day in March the fare from Kansas City was lowered to $10, then to $5, then for one wild moment to $1. Special cars were added, and freight cars were converted into kitchens to feed the incoming hordes. Weather was one lure; health, restored, was one advertisement.

These people came to stay. Within the decade the population of the city jumped to 55,000 residents, more than four times its 1880 number. Almost everyone was a brand-newcomer. Los Angeles welcomed the mobs; the growth of the city became almost a religious endeavor. Getting big was getting business; getting residents meant getting rich.

Nowadays the trains carry a much smaller number of incoming Americans; most new arrivals come by air. The "live steamers" at Griffith Park are for resident tourists, not for travelers.

Engineer Bart Sissons at the controls of a scale model train near Travel Town in Griffith Park

New towns with bright futures

Hollywood was born in 1887—the community, not the movie industry. Many new communities were also starting up in answer to the immense influx of people from other parts of the country. Azusa—A to Z in the USA—was established; Pomona was incorporated; Whittier was being settled by Quakers from the Midwest; and Glendale was started. Next door, the new city of Burbank was founded—without a hint that it was destined to become a kind of show-business capital for the next century, with huge studios belonging to Disney, Warner Brothers, and NBC.

God-fearing was the word for most of these new boom-born communities. The prohibitionists settled Hollywood, set their own rules, and lived by them: no booze, no pool parlors, no rowdyism. Little did a band of Kansas Protestants dream that their temperate, teetotal new home would become the universal word for movies, glamour, and gaudiness.

Hollywood—the entertainment industry, not the community—would settle in during the first decade of the twentieth century, establishing locations in Culver City, West Los Angeles, and Burbank as well as in Hollywood itself. The 1880s land rush, fueled by railroad rate wars and promoted by righteous immigrants, was later replaced by a show-biz explosion brought on by bright skies and temperate weather. The Disney operation in Burbank was probably the best bridge between family propriety and film promotion.

Film fantasy: Major Effects, *starring Joseph Bottoms, in the works at Disney Studios in Burbank*

Monuments in the making

As the decade of growth was nearing its end, the expansionist spree was collapsing in overspeculation, overextension of credit, and overconfidence. Even Lucky Baldwin, the big lender, could not pay his own employees for a time.

But Los Angeles managed to maintain some economic resiliency. Fort Street was widened in 1888 to accommodate a new City Hall. Sidewalks and streets were still being paved. Even collapse could not prevent the city from becoming a more civil place, a sounder and more permanent community.

The Triforium, a sixty-foot fountain for music built in 1975, stands as a symbol of civic optimism. The City Council appropriated $1 million for sculptor Joseph Young to create his multicolored concrete tower with speakers. It stands, usually mute, in the new city mall northeast of the present City Hall, itself an unusual example of architecture. The Triforium has inspired more controversial discords than chords in its short lifetime, an aesthetic argument perfectly suited to a city that has repeatedly tuned in to boom and adjusted to bust.

The Los Angeles Triforium, a musical landmark in a mall, with City Hall in the background

1889

Floral pageant as a real estate promotion

The Rose Tournament began as a pageant for Pasadena, a means of stimulating local pride in the wake of economic prosperity. Southern California would show the rest of America that it could bloom in January. Winter might mean sleet in Chicago and snow in New York; in Pasadena it produced showers of flowers. But back in 1889 the tournament was not even a regular parade; it merely featured chariot races.

Many students of Los Angeles history believe that the annual Rose Parade and Rose Bowl football game on January 1 produce more restless Americans than any other single event. While hundreds of thousands of Californians turn out on the balmy New Year to watch the parade and the game, tens of millions of housebound Americans get the message from television loud and clear—a warm climate rather than football scores is what really counts.

Pasadena's Rose Parade, biggest grandstand play in the nation

Public places in which to park

By 1890 Los Angeles had miles of paved streets and even miles of sidewalks on formerly bare earth. Los Angeles had evolved into a real city, although it still had problems of space and sewers and slapdash development.

William Workman, mayor of Los Angeles from 1886 to 1888, was sensitive to the changes. He had sponsored the pavings and had been a prime mover in setting up the library system. He realized that urban life required land for relief from concrete and asphalt. In 1890 Workman and Mrs. J. E. Hollen-beck donated land to the city in the beautiful residential area of Boyle Heights for the creation of Hollenbeck Park.

Hollenbeck is still a handsome park, but Boyle Heights, which is now a section of the East Los Angeles barrio, has deteriorated. The nearby freeway dispatches dirt—and decibels—to the greenspace. Los Angeles remains a city where the necessity for roads paved over too many good intentions.

Hollenbeck Park in Boyle Heights near the Golden State Freeway

An era of oranges

By the 1890s the orange was becoming the symbol of Southern California affluence, the gold that grows above ground and renews itself each season ripe for shipping. The Spanish had brought the orange to Southern California, and American pioneer William Wolfskill planted the first commercial orchard in 1841. Oranges grown in Southern California won prizes at an 1884 international exposition. But as a lucrative commercial endeavor the orange business was just beginning to make it big in the 1890s.

The railroad linkup with Santa Fe in 1886 made export of the citrus fruits more feasible. A refrigerator railroad car was developed in 1890. Southern California was on the verge of cashing in on its citrus crops. By 1891 citrus was the biggest industry in the region. Within the decade the number of acres planted to oranges increased fivefold to more than 5.5 million trees.

Charles Lummis, the man who walked cross-country to settle in California sunshine, once described the orange as a romance as well as a fruit. And Carey McWilliams noted in his book *Southern California: An Island on the Land:* "The orange tree is the living symbol of richness, luxury, and elegance. With its rich black-green shade, its evergreen foliage, and its romantic fragrance, it is the millionaire of all the trees of America, the 'golden apple' of the fabled garden of the Hesperides."

Citrus reigned supreme in the Los Angeles area until human growth began to crowd out the groves in the 1940s and the trees were razed to build tract houses. Today Los Angeles County has been squeezed out of the orange business; the major groves are in neighboring counties—Orange, Ventura, and Riverside.

Money grows on trees—to be picked and packed

Here comes the oil

Edward L. Doheny was a prospector who came to Los Angeles in 1892 and immediately began investigating stories about brea, the peculiar tar seeping out of the ground. Brea was once used by Indians to seal their boats and by early settlers to cover their adobe roofs. But Doheny had a more lucrative possibility in mind—he figured the tar came from underground oil pools.

Doheny purchased a lot in the residential neighborhood near the intersection of present Second Street and Glendale Boulevard and with help from Charles Canfield began digging. They sank a mine shaft and struck natural gas only seven feet down. The fumes made further digging by hand impossible. So they devised a drill out of eucalyptus wood and soon began bringing up buckets of oil.

Other people took notice and immediately started digging up their backyards; more than 600 wells were in operation before the turn of the century. In those days there was more oil than demand; the wells had come in before the automobile arrived.

(Overleaf) On the islands off Long Beach, drill rigs are camouflaged to look like high-rises

Beauty that outlasts prosperity

Los Angeles was not without its architectural masterpieces by 1893. Los Angeles architect Sumner Hunt had been commissioned to design an office building for mining tycoon Louis Bradbury. But Bradbury rejected Hunt's drawings; he asked one of Hunt's young apprentice draftsmen, George Herbert Wyman, to take on the project, even though Wyman lacked formal training. The young man, something of a mystic, initially declined the offer but then accepted after supposedly receiving a message from his dead brother.

The result is a drab orange brick exterior enclosing the most magical and magnificent interior in all of Los Angeles. Iron-grated elevators glide up the sides of the court beneath a skylit roof. Marble, glazed brick, rich woods, tiles, and wrought iron combine with sunlight to define a space studied even today by architects. Several design firms in fact have their offices in the Bradbury Building. Many motion pictures and television series have utilized the building as a glorious turn-of-the-century backdrop. Wyman's masterpiece is still effective.

But it was his first and final monument. Wyman took formal training after the Bradbury was built but never produced anything to match it.

A UCLA design class photographing the Bradbury Building

Los Angeles strikes it poor

Economic depression hit Los Angeles toward the middle of the 1890s. There was more oil pumped than was needed. The railroad workers went on strike, and, as a result, the glorious California oranges were not shipped to the rest of the country. Los Angeles was virtually cut off from the world in 1894; unemployed men were out on the streets, and there were labor riots.

What the town required was a tourist celebration, a pageant to distract from the resident poverty. The new Merchants Association sponsored the Fiesta de Los Angeles, a novel attempt to turn a profit from the old Spanish heritage and a promotion to divert the local population from the annual fair in San Francisco. Yet the depression continued, and by late spring government troops had to be called in to help ensure order as the strike continued.

The old Dominguez oil field, between downtown Los Angeles and Long Beach

Growth gets rolling again

Trains were rolling in 1895, bringing new residents. The influx extended neighborhoods and encouraged increased subdivision of the region. An electric street railway opened to Westlake Park, and William May Garland successfully sold lots in the new community. A branch of the Southern Pacific was extended to Pasadena the same year. An electric railway even climbed Mount Lowe, where Professor Thaddeus Lowe had built a fancy hotel.

Spencer Crump's history of Los Angeles trolleys, *Ride the Big Red Cars,* reprints one of William May Garland's ads tying real estate development to transportation. "Only six minutes from the heart of our city," read the copy. "Tract will contain only good homes, nothing objectionable permitted. Ride to this tract and look it over carefully. When the new Fourth Street bridge is built these lots will more than double in value." Garland was selling the lots for $300. He predicted a population of 250,000 by 1910, although there were fewer than 100,000 people in the mid-1890s. His prediction proved wrong; by 1910 Los Angeles had a population of more than 300,000.

MacArthur Park, former Westlake Park, viewed from the air with downtown Los Angeles in the background

1896

Where to have a harbor?

The fight over a suitable location for the major harbor in Los Angeles was still raging in 1896. When a visiting senator from Maine, William Frye, took a look at the suggested site at San Pedro, more than twenty miles from the city—and which would have to be a man-made deepwater port—he wryly noted: "Well, it seems you have made a great mistake in the location of your city. If you Los Angeles people want a harbor, why not move the city to San Diego? There is a good harbor there."

Collis Huntington, the rail king, wanted a harbor at Santa Monica. Captain John Ainsworth opted for one at Redondo Beach, where he had already constructed a wharf. Huntington and Harrison Gray Otis, publisher of the *Los Angeles Times,* carried the battle to Congress—Huntington claiming that San Pedro was impossible, Otis retorting that Santa Monica would only enrich Huntington. After days of debate in Washington, Senator Stephen White from California won the argument for San Pedro. By 1898 Congress approved an initial appropriation of $400,000 to begin work on a breakwater.

View of San Pedro, Los Angeles's harbor

1897

An overture to culture

The big news of 1897 was California's rank as third-largest oil-producing state in the nation. The last of the horse-drawn carts were disappearing from the streets, replaced by electric railways. Frank Wiggins, the biggest booster in town, was appointed secretary of the Chamber of Commerce, assuring his place in local legend: "God did much for Los Angeles, but Frank Wiggins did the rest."

Culture followed close on the heels of commerce. Amid the mechanical noises of the new prosperity echoed the sweet sound of an orchestra. The Los Angeles Symphony was established in 1897, the fifth symphonic orchestra in the United States and the first one west of the Rocky Mountains. Historian Lynn Bowman records that the debut tickets cost twenty-five cents while the fee paid each musician was fifty cents. Conductor Harley Hamilton chose Beethoven's First Symphony for the inaugural concert. Although there was not an oboe or a bassoon player available for the performance, Bowman claims that the audience didn't notice.

The present Los Angeles Philharmonic, complete with oboes and bassoons, is acclaimed as one of the major orchestras in the United States, regularly playing at both the Music Center and the Hollywood Bowl.

Los Angeles Philharmonic in rehearsal at the Music Center

The biggest public park in the United States

In 1898 Los Angeles got a public park for Christmas. It came from Griffith Jenkins Griffith, who made his fortune in mining as a geologist and a journalist reporting on properties from Nevada to Mexico. Griffith had settled in Los Angeles in 1882, buying up 4,000 acres of the old Los Feliz Rancho for $50,000 and opening a real estate office in town. By 1896 he was ready to make his big offer, more than 3,000 acres of Los Feliz land for public use, "as a Christmas gift."

Horace Bell, publisher of the crusading periodical *Porcupine,* made the claim that Griffith's generosity was only an attempt to avoid taxes. Local historian Boyle Workman later corroborated that claim. The city was slow to accept Griffith's donation, but in 1898 the deed was done and signed.

Griffith Griffith gave ground but remained a man of controversy. In 1903 he shot his wife in the eye, accusing her of trying to poison him. He went to jail for two years and then gave the city an observatory in the nation's biggest public park as another Christmas present.

A nature walk on the Griffith Park trails, high above Hollywood

Enter the automobile

The introduction of the horseless carriage, built in the East to reshape the West, supposedly occurred in 1899 when the folk of Los Angeles were induced to admire this new toy for rich men. A few years earlier a couple of local boys trying to make good had already rolled out a four-cylinder machine of their own and had driven their friends downtown.

The automobile arrived, making it possible to use up all that gasoline, to create urban sprawl, and eventually to undermine an established rapid transit system. It would become the symbol for the city as well as a local joke, a local love object, and literally a way of life. Within the next two decades Los Angeles would possess more automobiles than any other city in the world, a not-so-free-wheeling achievement that has remained on the record books ever since.

A present-day meeting of the Horseless Carriage Club of America, Southern California branch, at La Crescenta Park

1900

A century turns for the most-celebrated city in America

Los Angeles entered the twentieth century with a population of 102,000 and a special brand of homegrown optimism. The harbor was under way; factories in the region were turning out $21 million worth of goods for that year; a stock exchange was organized. The boosters had overcome extraordinary odds to achieve their success. If Northern California had developed out of Gold Rush fever, then Southern California did so out of reasoned opportunism—the people who came to Los Angeles came there with weather on their minds and money in the bank.

The Chamber of Commerce published more than two million flyers describing the rare beauties of Southern California. A train, christened *California on Wheels,* was sent through the Midwest and the South, bringing fancy fruits and seductive photographs. The city picked up the tab for visiting business groups and associations, offering them a free trip for a chance to induce them to relocate. Historian Carey McWilliams noted that "by 1900 Los Angeles was the best-advertised city in America." If water was scarce, if resources were rare, if distances were great, the bright sunshine was real and the flowers—blooming year-round—were magnificent. Magnificent too is the new advertisement to the outside world, the HOLLYWOOD sign, originally a symbol of real estate development but now rebuilt and rededicated to the principles of hoopla over humility.

Hollywood sign, high in the hills, is a symbol of celebration and self-advertisement

1901

A flight of Angels

By the 1900s many Los Angeles residents were living atop Bunker Hill in the downtown area. The business district was below, starting at Hill Street and extending to the east.

The inventive citizens of the city looked high and low in 1901 to bring commerce and community closer together. On high, Angels Flight, a wonderful little funicular railway on Third Street between Hill and Olive, connected the two districts. For over a half century, at the one-way fare of a penny, residents could ride this landmark funicular for one steep block. Below was a tunnel through Bunker Hill, along Third Street between Hill and Hope.

Beloved as Angels Flight may have been, the little train that could was untracked in the 1960s to make way for urban redevelopment. The city promised restoration as soon as Bunker Hill was rebuilt. But the hill was bulldozed and the tracks removed. The cars themselves, still in storage, do not meet present safety standards. The promise will most likely be fulfilled as a reconstructed rather than a restored Angels Flight—more a tourist attraction than a working train.

While the tunnel still remains at Third, Angels Flight exists in name only—as a revolving restaurant atop the Hyatt Regency Hotel.

Angels Flight cars in storage

And now to scrape the sky

Los Angeles had lived within a seven-story ceiling for decades. After the turn of the century it was high time to double building heights and create a new skyline. The Brady Building was designed by John Parkinson, the prominent architect who later had a hand in the Alexandria Hotel across the street, the Pacific Stock Exchange two blocks south, and City Hall, as well as Union Station nearly four decades later. The Brady, later renamed the Hibernian Building, is Beaux Arts in style but somewhat subdued compared with its historic neighbors.

Spring Street today is lined with sturdy old buildings, many of them vacant above street level. The former financial center suffers from the taint of Skid Row one block away on Main and from the exodus to the newer banking headquarters toward the west, where second-generation skyscrapers rise more than forty stories, reshaping the skyline along the Harbor Freeway.

The architecture also rises at Spring Street and Fourth

1903

A gallery, a garden, and a library that would become famous

In 1903 Henry Huntington bought the San Marino Ranch and began planting gardens, the beginning of a mammoth private cultural center. He was the nephew of the controversial Collis Huntington, superbaron of the Southern Pacific. Henry Huntington made his fortune with an extraordinary network of neighborhood trolley lines, the Red Cars.

In 1909 he began building a mansion for himself which would later become an art gallery, housing works by such artists as Gainsborough, Reynolds, and Constable. In 1919 in a separate building he began what would become one of the world's great libraries, concen-trating on British and American history from the eleventh century to the present.

The Huntington Library, Art Gallery, and Botanical Gardens first opened to the public in 1928, the year after Henry died. Spread over 207 acres, the complex today attracts international scholars, collectors, schoolchildren, and tourists. The library, perhaps America's finest residual benefit from the era of great railroad fortunes, offers both a center for scholarly research and entertainment for more casual visitors.

Student tour group entering Huntington Library in San Marino

1904

A staple from the sea

The fishing industry was just getting its start around San Pedro Bay, one of the earliest instances of Los Angeles attracting international enterprise. A group of Japanese arrived shortly after the turn of the century and began fishing for abalone. Yugoslavians and Italians came to fish for albacore. As early as 1903 Ed Young, an American, began bringing in a daily catch on his boat *Alpha*. Another American, Albert Halfhill, organized the Southern California Fish Company; by 1904 Halfhill was packing tuna, and a billion-dollar industry was on its way at Terminal Island.

Today the tonnage handled along Terminal Island's Tuna Street ends up at canneries packing albacore, bonito, mackerel, and sardines. The cosmopolitan mix of the cannery employees still exists, with Asians, Europeans, and Hispanics presently working the factories.

(Overleaf) A big catch unloaded at the cannery on Terminal Island

193

1905

An American Venice

Abbot Kinney dreamed of building a Venice of America, complete with canals, cultural entertainments, and an educated community. Kinney already had money from his family's Sweet Caporal cigarette company, and he was well educated; he even wrote books on philosophy and commerce. Kinney also had a social conscience; he contributed to Helen Hunt Jackson's work for the Indians and helped establish forest preserves.

Kinney had sixteen miles of waterways dredged south of Ocean Park. He commissioned Italian Renaissance architecture to be built on the site, imported singing gondoliers, set up an oriental art gallery, and sponsored a scientific aquarium.

But the public preferred less exalted amusements. In order to exist, Venice of America had to lower its sights from culture to carnival—it finally became another beach amusement park. Eventually it was annexed to Los Angeles, and by the 1950s the resort had been transformed into a haven for the poor, the beats, the old, and the artists. The canals deteriorated along with the neighborhood. Yet Venice rebuilds today, too close to the ocean to remain a backwater community.

Venetian canal in Southern California

1906

Rancho Rodeo de las Aguas becomes Beverly Hills

In 1906 the Rodeo Land and Water Company bought the old Rancho Rodeo de las Aguas, and the company's president Burton E. Green began thinking about a new name for the development. Green had read about a place called Beverly Farms in Massachusetts where U.S. President William Howard Taft frequently vacationed. Beverly sounded good, but Farms seemed too bucolic. So Green lifted his eyes to the Santa Monica Mountains and settled on Hills.

Beans and barley at Beverly Hills gave way to trees and trim bungalows. A landscape architect from New York, Wilbur Cook, created a plan of winding streets, and in 1915 the luxurious Beverly Hills Hotel was built on Sunset Boulevard north of the point where the winding roads came together. Wealthy people moved into the neighborhood—first professional or retired people, followed by the movie crowd, including Charlie Chaplin, Gloria Swanson, Harold Lloyd, and Tom Mix. Rancho Rodeo de las Aguas translated roughly as "where the waters meet"; Beverly Hills came to mean where the wealthy settled.

Beverly Hills, barely larger than five square miles when incorporated in 1914, today remains a small enclave of wealth completely surrounded by sprawling Los Angeles. It is still the center of the amusement business, where rock stars mingle with movie and television stars and where dealers and wheelers come to the Beverly Wilshire, the Beverly Hills, and the Beverly Hilton hotels to lounge poolside and package hits for the rest of America.

Poolside at the Beverly Hilton Hotel—from rainbows to riches

1907

Movies move in

Francis Boggs, a pioneer motion picture director, came to town in 1907. He had been making a one-reel version of *The Count of Monte Cristo* for William Selig in Chicago, but since scenes were all shot outdoors, good weather was a necessity. Boggs gave up on Chicago and went west in search of sunshine. He brought with him cameraman Thomas Persons; for financial reasons the cast had to be left behind in cold, cloudy Chicago.

Boggs and Persons hired a hypnotist to take over the role of the count, ignoring the problems of shooting a picture with two different actors playing the same leading role. For the climactic scene, where the count emerges from the sea, the hypnotist waded into the water wearing a great white wig. In the midst of the action a wave washed away the wig, and Boggs and Persons had to dive into the water to save both star and hair. *The Count* opened the following year—the first important picture filmed in California.

Mann's Chinese Theater, built as Grauman's in 1927—Hollywood's most famous palace for celebrating itself

1908

Pity and protect the poor pedestrian

In the first decade of the twentieth century the population of Los Angeles tripled, soaring from slightly more than 100,000 to nearly 320,000. And this expansive decade also saw more and more cars on the streets of Los Angeles—and more accidents too. In 1908 Captain John Butler, determining to do something to protect life against traffic, drew up the first traffic regulations for the city. For his vision as well as his dedication to the pedestrian, he was later rewarded by being appointed chief of police.

Stop signs appeared in 1923, and traffic lights were introduced in 1931, 150 years after the first forty-four settlers struggled up from Mexico.

Today at Century City and at overpasses in the Bunker Hill area the separation of pedestrian traffic from vehicular traffic is one of the modern methods of preventing people in cars from killing those on foot.

*Pedestrian overpass at
Century City*

Shoestring to sustain a city

Harbor construction had been under way at San Pedro for a decade. But Los Angeles was separated from its seaport by nearly twenty miles of county land. The city wanted to annex the harbor, and as early as 1907 the Chamber of Commerce established a Harbor Commission, an act of optimism somewhat like the Swiss navy hoping to set up bases on the Mediterranean. The plan was to annex land, moving progressively southward until Los Angeles was extended down to Wilmington just north of Terminal Island. The extension was only one mile wide, like a long fishing line, later called the shoestring strip. Then in 1909, amid more controversy, both Wilmington and San Pedro in separate elections decided to consolidate themselves as part of the city of Los Angeles.

The shoestring still exists, a thin strip of turf along the Harbor Freeway that extends from the center of the city to San Pedro, running between the communities of Inglewood, Compton, and Torrance on the way to the ocean.

Ships in Los Angeles Harbor

Aviation meets the angels

No one realized in 1910 that aviation would join oil and motion pictures as one of the great industries of Los Angeles. But there was plenty of curiosity at Dominguez Field, lying between the city and the harbor, when America's first international air show was staged that year. Over 50,000 people crowded the grandstands to gape at the biplanes and dirigibles and a demonstration of bombing in which sandbags were used instead of explosives.

Western Airlines, originally called Western Air Express, began mail service in 1926 and launched passenger service in 1928. During the 1920s there were more licensed planes and pilots in Los Angeles than in any other city in the country. For here was an almost irresistible combination of adventure, open space, and sunshine.

The other major event of 1910 was a real bombing, no sandbag demonstration, at the *Los Angeles Times*. Foundry workers were on strike, and the newspaper came out angrily against unions. The explosion took place on October 1; twenty people were killed, and the building was destroyed. The *Times* blamed "the vicious utterances of designing, unscrupulous union leaders." The McNamara brothers—John and James—were eventually convicted, despite a strong defense from lawyer Clarence Darrow.

Western Airlines, a pioneer passenger carrier, lands one of its planes at Los Angeles International Airport (multiple exposure photograph)

A bear flag for a state

The California legislature adopted a state flag in 1911—the Bear Flag, in tribute to the Bear Flag men who in the 1846 American rebellion against Mexico took over a section of northern California before the United States victory was complete. Today the Bear Flag flies among a number of other historic emblems at the Los Angeles County Mall.

The year 1911 marked further historic developments. Local railway lines were consolidated, the Pacific Electric coming under Southern Pacific control. Henry Huntington, the museum and library man, now dominated street transportation in town. In the burgeoning movie industry Thomas Ince, director of Mary Pickford for the Independent Motion Picture Company, decided to build a studio. He had seen a Wild West carnival and had a hunch that Western movies—featuring cowboys, Indians, and animals—could capture the imagination of America. His first headquarters was in the neighborhood of Echo Park; then he created Inceville, a complex backed up against the Santa Monica Mountains where Sunset Boulevard now ravels out to the sea.

(Overleaf) Second-grade students at Union Avenue Elementary School, near downtown Los Angeles, display colors

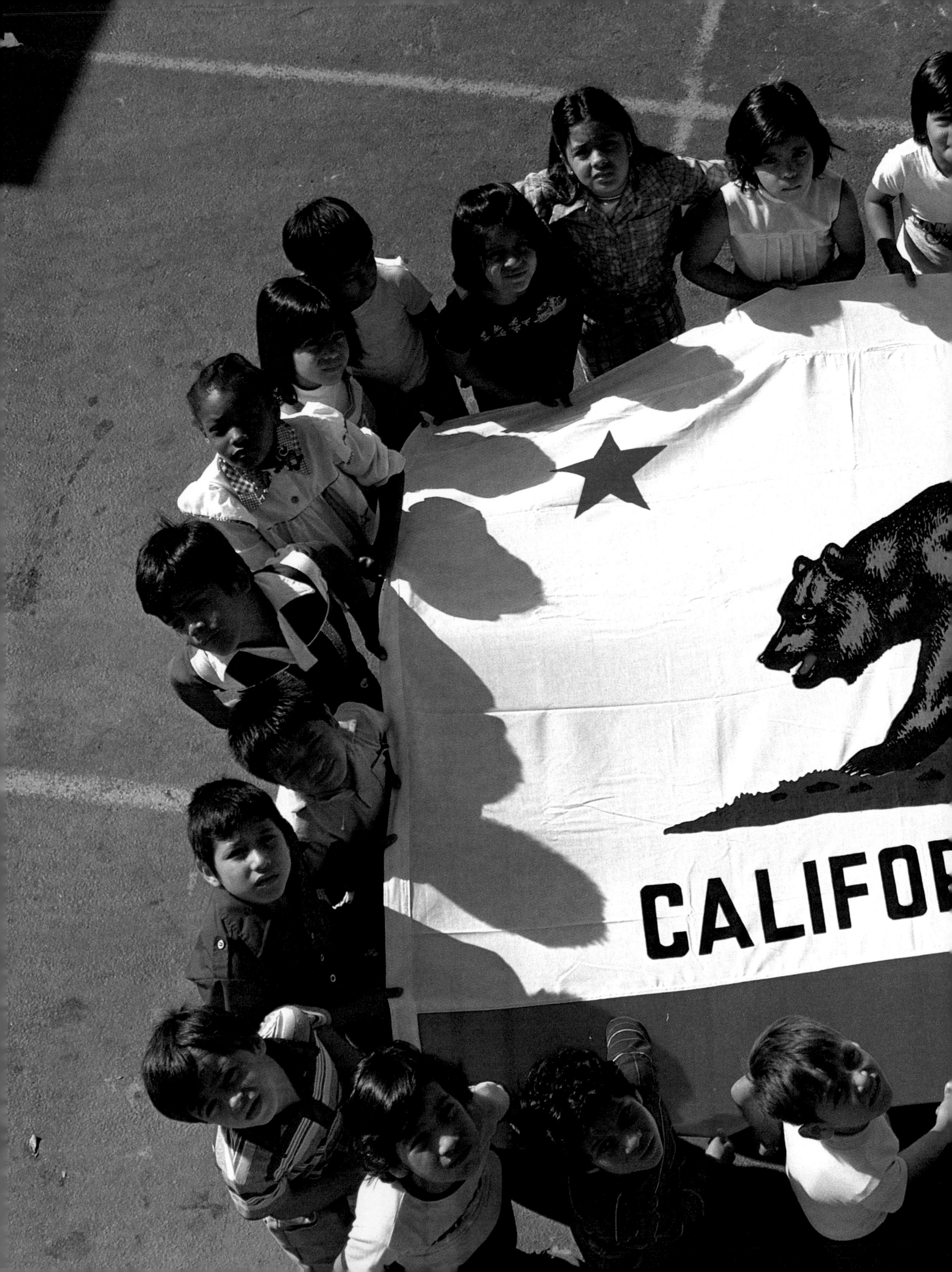
CALIFOR

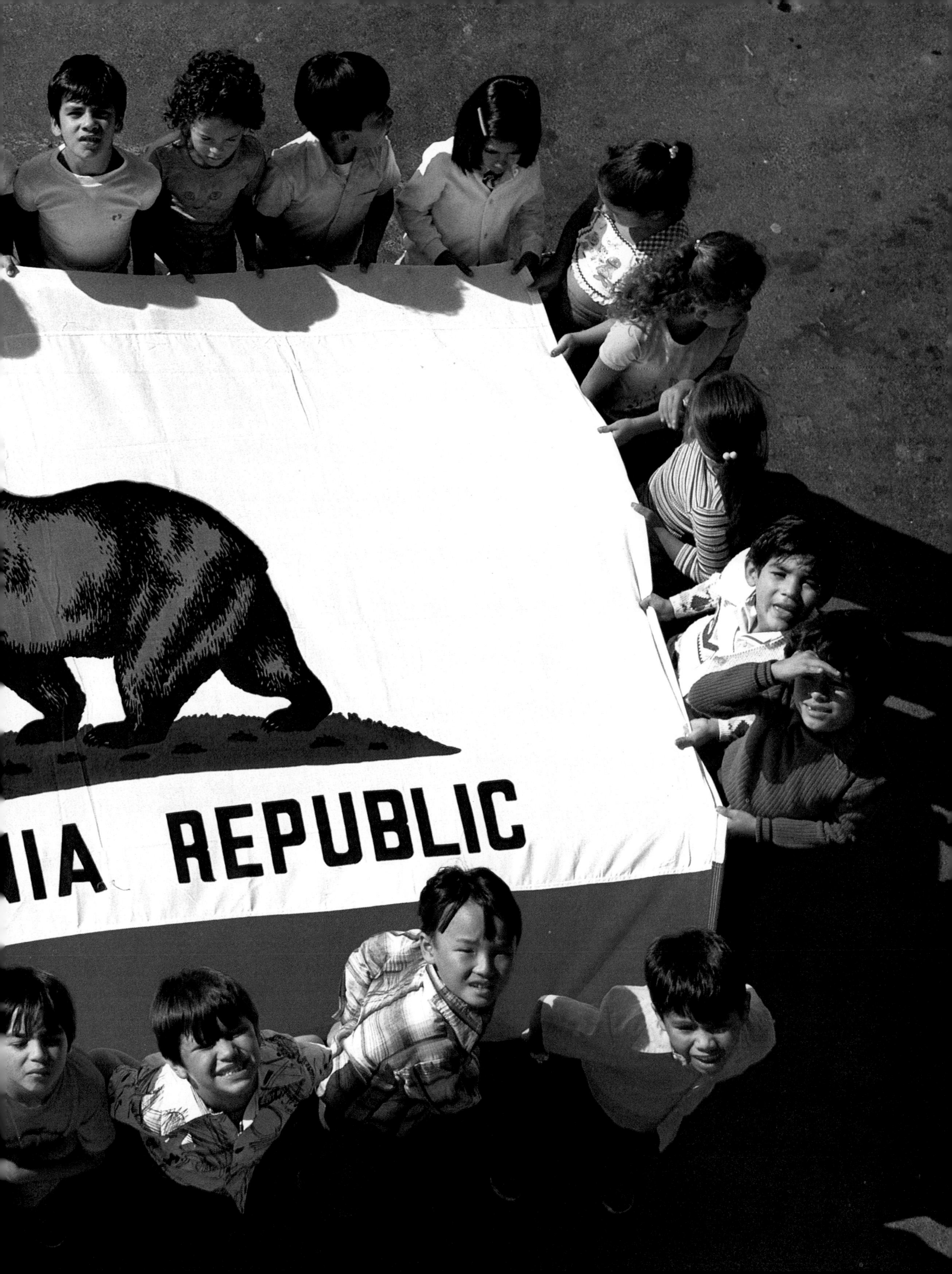
NIA REPUBLIC

A retreat for tired businessmen

A local athletic club was organized as early as 1880. By 1912 the members were ready to build their fifth—and current—home on Seventh Street. The attractions of the Los Angeles Athletic Club today are remarkably like those when it originally opened: a place to eat, swim, and exercise—privately— among peers. The club produced its share of champions in track and swimming, including Buster Crabbe, who later left Olympic pools for motion pictures to play Buck Rogers and Tarzan.

The downtown clubs of Los Angeles, including the Los Angeles Athletic Club designed by Parkinson & Bergstrom, have been designated historical landmarks. The Jonathan and California clubs offer food and conviviality to the poshest business interests in town. Robert Farquhar, architect for the California Club, created a magnificently detailed brown brick Beaux Arts building, a classic of its kind.

Snobbery competed with fellowship in the clubs. Only in recent years has social progress begun to keep pace with social standing.

Members of the Los Angeles Athletic Club playing rooftop paddle tennis above downtown

Waterflow follows demand

The controversy over San Pedro harbor seemed a mere spat compared with the larger water issue at the other end of town. From the beginning Los Angeles was a semiarid city at the mercy of sporadic rainfall, which accounted for years of growing green followed by harsh years of deadly drought. If the city was to sustain population growth and become a major American metropolis, something drastic had to be done to ensure a steady water supply.

The first big water importing project was begun by William Mulholland, who was appointed the first city Water Department superintendent in 1902, and Fred Eaton, a former mayor. In 1904 Eaton convinced Mulholland that the thousand lakes formed from Sierra snow melt in the Owens Valley could be tapped, if water rights could be purchased from local farmers. Eaton began buying up options, quietly dealing with individual farmers and suggesting that the sellers would benefit from a government irrigation project. When the farmers realized that they had sold their water down the river, they were furious. The farmers carried their protests all the way to President Theodore Roosevelt. But the aqueduct was under way.

Mulholland masterminded the effort, the most extraordinary engineering feat of the time: a project crossing more than 250 miles of desert and wilderness, including a five-mile tunnel bored through the Coast Range. On November 5, 1913, the aqueduct was completed. Over 40,000 people gathered at the Cascades to hear Mulholland utter his simple words of triumph as the water spilled into San Fernando Valley: "There it is—take it."

The aqueduct transformed San Fernando Valley into a more desirable basin for land speculation and set the pattern for later, even longer, water importation projects.

The Cascades, the last lap of the Owens River Aqueduct, flowing into northern San Fernando Valley

Bum start for busing

The jitney bus system in Los Angeles began in 1914, when a few enterprising business people figured there was demand for buses to carry citizens beyond the regular railway stops. But bus transit failed within the year; Huntington's Pacific Electric Railway—the Red Cars—was running all the way to Long Beach, and interurban rail traffic was all the city needed for decades. Buses were brought back to service in 1923, but, as John Weaver pointed out in *El Pueblo Grande,* "by then more than one-third of the city's commuters were driving to work in their own automobiles."

Only in the 1970s did bus transit begin to make economic sense again, given rising gas costs and shortages and the difficulties of retracking the city.

New Southern California Rapid Transit District bus bends around a downtown corner

"—And make the San Fernando Valley our home"

The campaign to annex San Fernando Valley into the ever-greater city of Los Angeles began in 1915 with a slogan: Put the aqueduct water to work at once. Voters were urged to endorse annexation on grounds of uniform city-set water rates and increased municipal revenue for improved power projects. The merger was approved, another in what seemed to be an annexation epidemic during the decade. When Los Angeles incorporated Hollywood in 1910, the city was less than 90 square miles; by 1920 it was nearly 364 square miles. The Valley annexation alone added 170 square miles.

In modern times San Fernando Valley has drastically changed from a farming region to a commuting center as thousands of tract houses replaced the orchards. By 1960 the population had soared to 850,000—multiplying five times in less than two decades. Just off Van Nuys Boulevard, a complex satellite civic center today services the Valley with police, courts, and community hearing rooms.

(Overleaf) A telephoto compression of commerce and chaos along Van Nuys Boulevard, major artery of San Fernando Valley

214

1916

A vamp is born

Theodosia Goodman was the original vamp, a word derived from vampire. She had already acted onstage as Theodosia De Coppett but became famous for her sex appeal under the new name of Theda Bara.

In 1914 William Fox was making a film entitled *A Fool There Was*, based on the stage play of the same name, which in turn had been adapted from Rudyard Kipling's poem "The Vampire." Director Frank Powell was impressed by the sultry, plump charm of Theodosia and renamed her Theda Bara, adapting her real first name and that of a relative named Barranger. *A Fool There Was* became a smash hit in 1915, and its star moved to California. By 1916 Theda Bara had starred in forty motion pictures—she was the prototype for a succession of sex queens, from Vilma Banky to Jean Harlow to Marilyn Monroe.

Carol Burnett brings vamping up to date at CBS Television City in costume by Bob Mackie and make-up by Joe Blasco

1917

A radical's park and Frank Lloyd Wright

Aline Barnsdall was one of Los Angeles's most liberated personalities. She campaigned for the freeing of India from British rule and erected huge billboards above Hollywood Boulevard, scandalizing the city fathers. On her own property she hoped to establish a kind of commune for women in the arts and politics. In 1917 she brought Frank Lloyd Wright to town to design her house, a synthesis of influences from midwestern prairie to Central American Mayan.

Wright also designed homes in Pasadena (1923), Hollywood (1923, 1924), and Brentwood (1939), lasting landmarks from the drawing board of the man who originated the notion of continental tilt—an explanation for the phenomena of all of the loose nuts from the rest of the United States sliding westward and eventually settling down in Southern California.

In 1927 Los Angeles took over the Barnsdall property as a park, although not without some hesitation since its owner had been a radical and an embarrassment. In 1967, with the help of the Junior League, the city established the Junior Arts Center at Barnsdall Park and in 1971 put up a municipal arts gallery on the Barnsdall grounds.

Five-year-old Trudy Regina Hales exhibits her self-portrait at Barnsdall Park Junior Arts Center

1918

Another tunnel to tomorrow

In 1918 Los Angeles felt the impact of World War I. The Southwestern Shipbuilding Company was organized to manufacture hulls for the Emergency Fleet Corporation; German citizens and purported Axis sympathizers were hauled off to internment camps; and local regiments were shipped out to become part of the American Expeditionary Force.

Even the emerging movie industry fell in step with the fervor of American patriotism. Cecil B. De Mille, at the age of thirty-six, tried to learn to pilot a plane, and Mary Pickford visited military bases—America's perennial sweetheart on the home front.

The brand-new tunnel along Second Street below Bunker Hill made downtown Los Angeles more accessible to commuting from the west—another proof of modern technology's ability to tame topography for the sake of growth.

Second Street Tunnel, a light at the end of World War I

1919

A bowl of music for the basin

In 1919 the new Theater Arts Alliance found in the Hollywood hills a place to perform "the finest forms of the arts and crafts and individual talents" as well as to promote community spirit, patriotism, "beautiful creations, and productions of every sort." H. Ellis Reed had been delegated to search for such a site, and with his father, William, he tromped over an area known as Daisy Dell in Cahuenga Pass. The two Reeds shouted at each other from hilltop to hilltop and discovered superb acoustics in the natural amphitheater. By means of pledge and promise, the Arts Alliance bought the property in 1919, and contralto Madame Anna Rozena was the first performer to test the acoustics of the newly constructed Hollywood Bowl. The first full performance was probably given on August 10, 1919, under the direction of Leopold Godowsky, Jr.

There were no seats in the early years; audiences sat on hillside grass. The stage was an old barn door. Again by public subscription, and by the fund-raising endeavors of citizens like Mrs. Artie Mason Carter, a permanent outdoor theater, including a bandshell, was soon built.

Hollywood Bowl retains its superb natural acoustics, muffled only by the nearby roar of the Hollywood Freeway.

A preconcert picnic feast at Hollywood Bowl; foreground, left to right: David Knight, Linda Knight, Buzz Bartholomew; background: Kathleen Rowsey, Jeffrey Peterson, Kitty Bartholomew

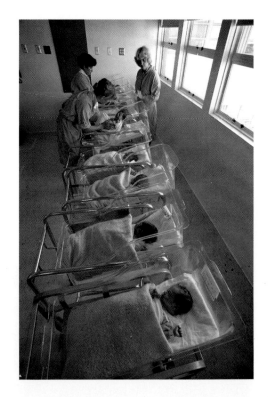

1920

A big city a-borning

At the beginning of a new decade the count in Los Angeles came to more than 575,000. The surrounding county boasted nearly twice that number.

Almost everybody was convinced that growth was important, in terms of both immigration from other parts of the country and local annexation of adjoining lands. The shoestring to the harbor had proved that an aggressive inland city could make its own way to water. The Owens River Aqueduct had shown that a resourceful semiarid city could buy its right to irrigation. The aqueduct had transformed San Fernando Valley from agricultural open space to a place for intense residential speculation and settlement. Private fortunes were being made as a result of this growth. And public projects were being financed because of increased economic activity.

Los Angeles had quite rapidly become the seventh-largest city in the United States—despite two major drawbacks, its great distance from large eastern cities like New York and Washington and its encirclement by mountains and deserts. Los Angeles had its own oil and its own illusions, minerals in the ground and movies on the screen.

Optimism is still strong, as evidenced by the city's continual delight in pace and place and physical pleasure. Even with its overdependence on the automobile—and with the accompanying smog—Southern California remains the place to go for fun and beauty.

Newborn babies at Los Angeles County General Hospital

1921

Success and scandal, as life imitates art

Everything seemed possible in 1921. The All-Year Club of Southern California was busy promoting tourism to the status of an industry. Stars were moving from Hollywood to the new palmier suburb of Beverly Hills. *The Sheik,* Rudolph Valentino's epic romance in the sand, was thrilling audiences everywhere. Movies were responsible for Los Angeles's growing reputation as the most glamorous, most affluent place in the American sun.

And then there was trouble in paradise. Roscoe Arbuckle, better known as "Fatty" for his 300 pounds, became as famous for a real-life sex scandal as he was for his rollicking screen comedy. He threw a wild party for his friends at which a young actress died. Arbuckle was accused of manslaughter, amid hints of orgy, perversion, and brutality. After three trials Arbuckle was acquitted of the killing, but his career as the lovable fat man of films was finished.

When director William Desmond Taylor was murdered in 1922 and, later, matinee idol Wallace Reid died of drug overdoses, it became evident that off-screen excess was one of the perils of Hollywood success. Movie censorship was right around the corner.

During these early scandal-ridden years, motion picture illusion was moving off the movie sets and into real life. The Spadena House is an example of fanciful residential architecture not uncommon in Los Angeles. It was designed in 1921 for a film and later was transported from the studio lot to a street in Beverly Hills where it has been occupied ever since, a gingerbread cottage in the style of Hansel and Gretel worth more than $500,000 in the fantasy market of real estate today.

The Spadena House, relocated from a movie set to Beverly Hills

1922

Farther west to Westwood

As bedrooms crowded the lima beans out of Beverly Hills, a new subdivision of Los Angeles, still farther west, was opening up. In 1922 the Janss Investment Corporation was offering lots for less than $1,000 and exhorting potential customers to buy quickly before prices doubled and quadrupled the way they had downtown.

Westwood Village developed as a kind of model community. The commercial center was designed around a triangle, neatly framed by whitewashed brick buildings with red tile roofs imported from Spain. Before the end of the decade, the University of California at Los Angeles chose Westwood as the new home for its campus.

Westwood still calls itself Village, despite its high-rise office buildings and apartment houses along Wilshire Boulevard, its multilevel underground parking lots, and its dozens of fast-food restaurants. The so-called village is the new center for urban-style movie theaters, jeans shops, and sidewalk nightlife. Twice a year Westwood closes its streets around the old triangle, inviting artists and craftspeople to traffic the area in place of the automobile. The original village life may now be overrun and overwhelmed but a bit of pedestrian pleasure has been preserved.

(Overleaf) Jenny Alkins and Michele Sachs sell Milar helium-filled balloons at a semiannual street fair in Westwood

Now up the hills into Bel-Air

Above the sounds of construction in Westwood, Bel-Air was taking over even higher ground in 1923. This subdivision was the brainchild of Alphonzo Bell: big lots, bigger than in the flatlands of Beverly Hills; lush landscaping, more luxurious than anything yet planted along the slopes of the Santa Monica Mountains.

A new land rush was in the making, and Bel-Air would become the most exclusive area in all of Los Angeles. Architect Mark Daniels planned most of the community in the 1920s. The winding streets were named with more than a hint of Old World charm and romance: Perugia, Chalon, Stradella, Siena. Gates were built to assure privacy and suggest prestige.

Bel-Air retains its reputation of exclusive elegance. While Beverly Hills is incorporated as a separate city, Bel-Air is a part of Los Angeles proper, perhaps its choicest area in terms of property value and snob appeal. Many estates sell for multiples of $1 million, even after the disastrous fire of 1961 when nearly 500 homes and more than 6,000 acres were reduced from affluence to ashes.

Real estate agents Deirdre Daniels and Jeff Hyland put their stakes into the rich soil at the West Gate of Bel-Air

The sky is no limit

The clamor for land unexpectedly subsided in 1924. Banks tightened credit, and property sellers outnumbered buyers. Los Angeles, a city of one million residents, had 45,000 real estate agents —most of them abruptly out of clients.

But there was still an excitement in the air. The enthusiasm for the fledgling aviation industry that began with the big international meet at Dominguez in 1910 continued through the 1920s. The generally clear Los Angeles weather was conducive to fine visibility. Little airports opened along the city streets, and everyone wanted to be a pilot. Donald Douglas opened his aircraft-manufacturing plant in 1916, as did Allen and Malcolm Loughead (who later changed the company name to the more phonetic spelling of Lockheed). John K. Northrop, who worked for the Lougheads and for Douglas during the 1920s, later built his own aviation empire.

In 1924 four World Cruisers built by Donald Douglas left Clover Field in Santa Monica for the first around-the-world flight. Planes from other nations had already tried and failed to circumnavigate the globe, but three of the Douglas craft completed the circle in six months, three years before Charles Lindbergh made his solo flight across the Atlantic. The world was rapidly shrinking, with Los Angeles one of the first places to put on the squeeze.

Federal Aviation Administration air controller Dave Ross monitors the plane traffic at Los Angeles International Airport

1925

*The canals of Venice
connect to the city*

In 1925, with a reluctant declaration of dependence, Venice allowed itself to be annexed by the larger city of Los Angeles. Abbot Kinney's dream of turning Venice into California's cultural center was to be a dream deferred.

Later in the 1920s offshore oil was discovered, and with drill rigs spotting the coast, oil production for a time became the most profitable development. For the next forty years Venice of California deteriorated steadily. In the late 1950s the beat generation settled in; during the late 1960s the hip wing of the youth movement took up residence. At last in the 1970s local pride in the community emerged and the forming of a town council was the natural outcome. The elderly, the blacks, the poor, the extremely wealthy —all the residents of the Venice peninsula—would finally make a concerted effort to merge their aspirations for a better life.

One of the modern devices for scaling traffic to simple human needs is the Venice bike path, a concrete ribbon bordering the beach, where a daily parade of cyclists marks the community's return to middle-class stability and the 1980s pursuit of fitness.

*Public bikeway along Venice
Beach*

1926

Sister Aimee sinks from sight

Aimee Semple McPherson, the reigning queen of Los Angeles's evangelists, had first attracted a flock of followers in San Diego in 1918 by staging revival meetings in a boxing arena and dropping divine messages from an airplane. In 1922 Sister Aimee fluttered into Los Angeles with her International Church of the Foursquare Gospel, ready to heal the sick, convert the pagans, and redeem the fallen.

She was a smash hit. She raised $1.5 million to build the Angelus Temple in Echo Park, with 5,000 seats for the faithful. She started her own magazine, *The Bridal Call*. She owned a brass band and a radio station, and she set up her own school for evangelists. Sister Aimee was the perfect preacher for the extravagances of the movie capital, the ideal minister for a town of transients. If blatant show biz was her method, salvation was her act.

In May 1926, at the peak of her success, Aimee disappeared—straight off the sands at Ocean Park. The city mourned her drowning, and a chartered airplane scattered flowers over her watery grave. A disciple died trying to locate her body at the bottom of the sea.

A month later Aimee reappeared at the Mexican border and claimed she had been kidnapped. The faithful hailed it as a miracle, the huge crowd that met her at the railroad station was the biggest gathering in the history of the city.

But when the press started asking questions about her kidnapping ordeal, Sister Aimee's story began to collapse. Instead of being lost at sea or trapped by felons, she apparently had been on a romantic idyll with a former worker from the temple. She was arrested and put on trial for interfering with justice and bearing false witness. Aimee was acquitted, but her glory was forever tarnished. The angel of the City of Angels died in 1944 from an overdose of sleeping pills.

A contemporary lady vanishes in the Pacific Ocean

No faster than forty

A new California law in 1927 established a maximum automobile speed of forty miles an hour on the open highway. If the sky was no limit, traffic on land had to be controlled.

Restraints in other areas were being imposed at the same time. Oil tycoon C. C. Julian, an advertising wizard, had already been exposed as more con artist than capitalist, having bilked nearly 50,000 investors in a mammoth stock swindle. More than $150 million of other people's money was lost in 1927 when trading in Julian stock was finally suspended. The Julian episode foreshadowed the 1929 stock market crash that preceded the Great Depression.

Jet landing at Los Angeles, a city of limits

A point of pride

Los Angeles's City Hall was a small adobe building when California became the thirty-first state in 1850. Government moved to larger quarters made of brick in the 1880s and then relocated during that decade to an even bigger building on Broadway.

By the 1920s it was obvious that Los Angeles had outgrown its headquarters. A team of architects—John Austin, John Parkinson, Albert C. Martin, and Austin Whittlesey—was commissioned to draw up plans for a new City Hall worthy of Los Angeles. They designed a building which was itself a point of pride, an unusual tapering tower with overtones of Greek and Egyptian styles. Their building was to be twenty-eight stories, the only structure in town allowed to rise above 150 feet (a limit imposed to minimize destruction during earthquakes and fires). The cost to taxpayers was almost $5 million, but the building turned out to be something of a bargain, since the architects and contractors managed to bring it to completion in 1928 at several thousand dollars below budget— a historic feat for any age.

Los Angeles's City Hall, viewed from the First Masonic Temple at the Plaza

A new place for public education
The first college in Los Angeles was Saint Vincent's (now Loyola-Marymount University), opened in 1865. By the turn of the century the University of Southern California, Occidental College, Pomona College, Redlands, Whittier, and Throop Polytechnic Institute (now Cal Tech) had opened as private halls of higher education.

The University of California at Los Angeles (UCLA) was established as a state teachers college on Vermont Avenue, where Los Angeles City College still holds classes. The state normal school became part of the state university in 1919, and by the 1920s the need for a new campus was pressing. For $1 million the university was offered approximately 400 acres at Westwood, where the Janss development firm was selling new lots. The money was raised by bond issues, and by 1929 the first buildings opened their doors in the midst of dirt and mud.

UCLA is now a mammoth institution, with professional schools, a medical center, research institutions, and an enrollment of nearly 30,000 students. Academically UCLA compares well with the parent California campus at Berkeley. In athletics UCLA competes with the private University of Southern California at Exposition Park.

The Franklin Murphy Sculpture Garden at UCLA north campus

1930

Depression in Beverly Hills—not so bad

The Great Depression had staggered most of America, but Beverly Hills was still bragging about its growth and prosperity. Within the decade the proud little city showed a population increase of 2,487 percent. That was taken to be an American record, and nobody could prove otherwise. Beverly Hills later boasted a bank that stayed open during the worst days when Franklin Roosevelt declared a bank holiday for financial institutions unable to pay their depositors in the midst of economic collapse.

Beverly Hills today remains one of the richest little cities in the United States. Hundreds of movie stars and their doctors and lawyers live in style along the curved streets between the boulevards of Sunset and Santa Monica. The most elegant shops of the world have branches on famed Rodeo Drive, and dozens of banks, brokerage houses, and financial institutions are located between Santa Monica and Wilshire. The investors of Beverly Hills are so busy going about their frantic business that few of them look up to enjoy the canopy of stained glass ornamenting the roof of Glendale Federal Savings at the broad intersection of Beverly Drive and Wilshire.

Palm trees reach toward stained-glass roofline of Glendale Federal Savings

1931

Jumping-off place for those depressed by the Depression

The bridge over Arroyo Seco, the great dry gulch in Pasadena, became in the early 1930s a jumping ground of last resort as despair gripped the country during the Depression.

The death count from Suicide Bridge totaled seventy-nine before the local government discovered an effective way to protect citizens from their own self-destruction. The city of Pasadena was spending $20,000 a year—a major item on the budget in hard times—for a special bridge patrol to prevent suicides. Then the city built a great barbed-wire fence on both sides of the bridgeway, which forced the would-be jumpers to search for other suitable places.

The sharply pointed steel fingers above Suicide Bridge today curve in toward the road, performing a similar preventive function.

Suicide Bridge in Pasadena

Olympics in Los Angeles

A welcome diversion during the Depression was the Olympics. Los Angeles was lucky to have them in 1932. If people couldn't go to work, they could go to the games. The Coliseum was enlarged to seat 105,000 people, making it the biggest stadium in the world. An Olympic Village was constructed in Baldwin Hills to house the visiting teams. Both foreign and Olympic flags were flying throughout the town.

The Coliseum was sold out when the games opened in July. Athletes from all over the world broke most of the previous records for performance, four of them setting new ones during opening day. Exposition Park became the shining star of the sports universe for a few days in 1932.

The Olympic Games are scheduled to return to Los Angeles in 1984, thanks to the international lobbying of attorney John Argue and Mayor Tom Bradley. The citizens are both pleased and apprehensive. They are anxious about the cost of the games, despite local legislation protecting taxpayers against Olympian debt. They worry about international incidents now that the games have become tied up with world politics. And, amid summer humidity and smog, they are even concerned about the quality of air that athletes and tourists as well as residents will be breathing.

At the peristyle entrance to the Los Angeles Memorial Coliseum, site of the 1932 Olympic Games, four men who helped bring the Olympics back to Los Angeles for 1984: attorney John Argue, with torch; Bill Schroeder, director of Citizens Savings Athletic Foundation, wearing 1932 boxing trunks; Perry O'Brien, former Olympic champion shot-putter and broadcaster; Jim Hardy, Coliseum general manager, in business suit

Natural disaster follows financial collapse

The time was 5:54 P.M. on March 10, 1933, when a massive earthquake hit Los Angeles. Its center was at Long Beach, but tremors spread to the surrounding communities as well as to Los Angeles itself. The Richter scale recorded 6.3—a major quake. Buildings tumbled. Streets split and caved in. Schools cracked apart. Fortunately the children had already left for home from the two dozen seriously damaged schools. More than 120 people were killed, and over $60 million worth of construction was turned to rubble. The United States Marines were called to the shores of Long Beach as part of the rescue force.

Earthquakes and hard times sometimes occur together. The 1933 quake hit the Los Angeles area at the height of the Great Depression. The mammoth 1971 quake in San Fernando Valley, 6.4 on the Richter scale, came during a year of recession and high unemployment.

The lessons of the shakes were not lost on building authorities. State construction codes today emphasize quake resistance. California engineers have developed building techniques to protect against earthquakes; these have been copied in other quake-prone areas of the world. California seismologists have studiously analyzed methods of quake prediction, but the state is as heavily crisscrossed by fault lines as it is by freeways. No mortal has yet figured out a means of quake prevention on this piece of earth that doesn't always stand still.

(Overleaf) Downtown Los Angeles in simulated earthquake caused by shaking the camera

1934

Optimism against the odds—Santa Anita Racetrack opens

In 1934 ground was broken in Arcadia for the building of Santa Anita, an elegant racetrack designed for owner Gerald Pidge by architect Gordon Kaufmann. Racetrack betting had been legalized in 1933, over the vociferous objections of clergymen and the writers at the *Los Angeles Times*. The *Times* had editorialized: "California has tried open racing and open gambling and the experience was worse than merely unsatisfactory. They are not prosperity-makers. Nor is the atmosphere that surrounds the average track a wholesome one."

But 1933 had been a particularly hard year. Repeal of Prohibition was effected nationally, allowing the use of alcohol as consolation against the personal despair of the Depression. And track betting was instituted locally, an opportunity for chance gain amid grim unemployment.

When Santa Anita opened in late 1934, 39,000 bettors and sightseers showed up. They continue to play at Santa Anita and at Hollywood Park, two of the most lavishly landscaped tracks in America.

Starting gate at Santa Anita

Epic, utopia, and art moderne

Approximately 4,000 unemployed Americans were arriving in Los Angeles each month in 1935. Optimism seemed to be nourished by sunshine, and utopian ideas were exported from California by the carload during the Depression. Dr. Francis Townsend had one such notion. In order to bolster the sick economy, he proposed to have a monthly check sent to every retired citizen provided that the check be cashed and spent promptly. By 1935 Townsend's headquarters was collecting more than $500,000 a year in nickels and dimes from Americans who accepted the plan as sound economic medicine.

The plan was never adopted, nor was the technocracy movement—the basis for it—ever more than a promise. Also rejected was Upton Sinclair's EPIC platform (End Poverty in California) on which the muckraking author unsuccessfully ran for governor in 1934.

Although unemployment was on the rise in Los Angeles, aircraft plants were expanding at the same time. A local NBC executive was predicting that television would soon usher in a new period of prosperity. And Pan-Pacific Auditorium, an elegant example of optimism in architecturally streamlined terms, was designed by Wurdeman & Becket. It opened in 1935, down the street from Farmers Market, where local produce growers had set up their stalls.

The land around Pan-Pacific is now being transformed into a public park. But the old facade may be preserved, a brave face from a more difficult era.

Pan-Pacific Auditorium, stream-lines preserved

1936

Shut the gates, close the borders

Boosterism had come home to roost with a vengeance. Hordes of people were stampeding into the Los Angeles basin looking for work or relief. By 1936 more than a million Californians were on public relief, 400,000 of them in Los Angeles County alone.

The police chief came up with a shrewd idea. He would station policemen at the eastern borders of the state to keep out "bums, crooks, and won't-works." The slightly more polite terms for the incoming masses were "indigents" and "undesirables."

The proposal was effective, at least for a couple of months. On some days the border patrol turned away as many as 1,000 would-be immigrants. But the idea was as clearly unconstitutional as it was cruel. The governor ordered the patrol off the borders, reminding the authorities in Los Angeles of the citizen's right to free movement within America.

Present-day immigration problems are between southern California and Mexico. Poverty to the south has induced hundreds of thousands of Mexicans to look for work or relief in the United States. Many of them have crossed the national border illegally, and although many of these illegal aliens have become hard-working residents, many have added to whatever other poverty problems exist in Los Angeles. The Constitution offers no guarantees for Mexicans who immigrate without papers. But there are profound humanitarian issues involved —and there are also economic advantages, for both the immigrants and the city, derived from the flood of unauthorized crossings.

Downtown Broadway, a pedestrian shopping mecca for Mexicans, many of them citizens but many of them undocumented immigrants

1937

Tracks toward rapid transit

Streamliner service between Los Angeles and Chicago was started in 1937 with a luxury Santa Fe train called the Super Chief, powered by a diesel locomotive. Southern Pacific had already initiated streamline trains between San Francisco and Los Angeles. There were even discussions about a rapid transit system being established within the sprawling city. A state planning board sent a proposal to Washington, requesting $93 million to erect elevated trainways and elevated roadways for buses to facilitate transporting masses of people across southern California. The impracticality of the automobile—in terms of traffic and space —was becoming more and more apparent.

But the seductive nature of automotive transit—offering privacy and self-determined schedule—has won out. The express busway along the San Bernardino Freeway, with a terminal designed by Daniel, Mann, Johnson & Mendenhall, was not in use until the 1970s. And intracity train service remains a proposal to alleviate the congestion of this community of sprawling freeways.

Overpass atop the San Bernardino Freeway near California State University, Los Angeles, providing pedestrian access to a rapid busway built along the center lanes of the freeway

1938

*Out of money, out of luck,
about at bottom*

The city was never in worse shape than it was in 1938. Scandal erupted in the police department; two officers were charged and convicted of killing a man who was slated to testify against the mayor. Worse scandal shook City Hall; Mayor Frank Shaw was implicated in vice and corruption. A special recall election was held in September. Shaw was voted out of office, and Fletcher Bowron came in on a reform platform. But there was a lack of funds in the treasury, and city employees had to be paid in scrip right after the recall election.

There was no place to go except up—or perhaps the movies. The film industry did not suffer during the Depression; motion pictures were a cheap and enticing means of escape. Radio also flourished; in 1938 six Hollywood stations spent a total of more than $18 million to employ actors and to pay staff salaries. Real business was in dire shape, but show business helped hold the city together.

Man passed out in a city parking lot

1939

Last of the great train terminals
The grand railway station had been under construction for five years. When it was finished in May 1939, over 500,000 curious citizens came to gape and gawk. Union Station had sixteen tracks, spacious parking lots, and lovely landscaping; six design teams had produced a handsome structure with a Spanish-style roof and modern open interiors. Union Station—serving the Santa Fe, Southern Pacific, and Union lines—was a final celebration of a dying breed; it was the last great passenger railway terminal built in the United States.

The railroads were in financial trouble even before opening-day ceremonies. Depression layoffs had cut personnel by half; more than half the route systems were losing money or had already gone bankrupt.

Today Union Station faces further economic troubles. Neither the reorganization of Amtrak nor the energy shortages have brought transcontinental train travel back in any significant way to its former prosperity. Los Angeles's trainmen sit in the vast lobby, almost alone, waiting to make one of the few daily runs.

Union Station, an imposing synthesis of Spanish and modern streamline design; brakeman John Brown and conductor Clarence Tangen wait for their run

A freeway way of life

The proposal for a parkway between Pasadena and Los Angeles had seemed logical, even necessary, since the 1920s. Some people were worried, even then, about a concrete eyesore spun out between the two communities. Others were afraid of the danger to human life. But most people simply wanted a faster way to get from the big city to the pretty suburb. By 1936 the councils for both towns approved the plan for a limited-access highway across South Pasadena. By 1938 ground was broken, and by 1940 the $5 million roadway was completed, at the same time that the Los Angeles population reached more than 1.5 million.

The Pasadena Freeway was an instant success—a target of Bob Hope jokes on radio, a blessing for commuters, a prototype of express roadways to come. Reyner Banham, a British architectural critic, later cited the Los Angeles free-way system as "one of the greater works of man."

Freeways do offer benefits in their own wide way. But they also divide neighborhoods while they encourage sprawl. They become the roadbeds where smog is created, and they cost fortunes to build. Los Angeles residents began to realize such roads were paved with problems by the 1960s, when freeways were no more than a few miles away from every home. By the 1970s people who had once claimed that they simply could not live in Los Angeles without the freeways were beginning to wonder whether they could continue to live with them.

Pasadena Freeway, approaching Los Angeles

1941

An army of airfoils

By 1941 Los Angeles had become the national capital of defense industries. At the beginning of the year companies in Los Angeles County were working on orders totaling $550 million, half of the California defense business and more than any similar-sized region in the country. Northrop, North American, Lockheed, Douglas, Hughes, and other companies were riveting airplanes. Shipyards were welding naval vessels. And local residents were changing their roles: actor James Stewart became a private in the army, and thousands of women went to work in defense plants. Rosie the Riveter was inducted into the defense industry, and the great American assembly line at last included both sexes.

For the United States, World War II started in December, and aircraft production broke all previous American records.

Assembly line at Northrop Corporation, building F-5 supersonic fighter-trainers for more than twenty nations

1942

A symbolic strike back

Jimmy Doolittle was a teenager when he came to California for the mammoth international air meet of 1910. The event made a great impact on him and changed the direction of his life. He eventually earned a degree in mining engineering and a doctorate in aeronautical engineering. In 1942 he was a lieutenant colonel in the Army Air Corps at a time when the war in the Pacific was going badly for the United States—following Pearl Harbor, the Philippines had been lost to the enemy early in the year and there were a number of defeats on the Pacific Islands.

The United States sorely needed an offensive victory, if not on land then in the air. On April 18, 1942, Doolittle, already in his mid-forties, led a swarm of sixteen B-25s off the aircraft carrier *Hornet,* nearly 690 miles from Tokyo. They dropped 500-pound bombs on Japan's capital as well as on Kobe and Nagoya. A stunning feat in conception and execution, the raid was a turning point in American confidence.

After the war Doolittle directed the Space Technology Laboratory in Southern California. Today he leads a quiet life in Santa Monica, an octogenarian still fascinated by engineering achievements and aerospace invention. The ancient and historic B-25 is kept in skyworthy condition for air meets and exceptional reunions such as the one photographed at Van Nuys.

Retired general James Doolittle in the cockpit of a B-25 bomber, owned by Challenge Publications, at Van Nuys Airport

1943

*An ugly domestic
war in the streets*

Thousands of sailors were stationed in Los Angeles during the hot summer of 1943, waiting for assignment to the war in the Pacific. They knew they would encounter dangers at sea, but they went looking for trouble before departure. Young Mexican-Americans had adopted a peculiar urban costume called the zoot suit—long coat, baggy pants tapering dramatically to pegged legs, and dangling chain; they were the most visible targets for the servicemen's frustration. The sailors usually started the fights, first at a ballroom in Ocean Park and later in the Mexican neighborhoods of East Los Angeles. Local police, perhaps rationalizing their actions through patriotism or blinded by bigotry, often watched the sailors club zoot suiters, and then moved in to arrest the victims. A race war, as senseless as it was ugly, had spilled into the streets of Los Angeles. Only when naval authorities marked the city as off-limits for men on leave did the fighting stop.

Zoot Suit, the 1978 play by Luis Valdez, focused on those difficult days. It was a major hit in Los Angeles but a failure in New York. Thomas Sanchez's 1978 novel *The Zoot-Suit Murders* centered on the same battleground and enjoyed its own success.

Actors Edward James Olmo, in hat, and Enrique Castillo from the cast of the Los Angeles production of Zoot Suit

The awesome wrong
of Japanese relocation

American citizens of Japanese ancestry had been interned in 1942; they did not begin to return home until December 1944, after the U.S. War Department's determination that the West Coast was no longer in imminent danger. The American panic born of prejudice would be a nagging memory for decades. During the war years German-Americans in New York were allowed to go about their everyday business.

In California, however, more than 110,000 people—two-thirds of them American citizens—were sent to relocation centers, as they were officially called, on orders from President Franklin D. Roosevelt. The ostensible reason was the fear of sabotage and a second Pearl Harbor on the West Coast.

Santa Anita Racetrack became the center for assembling Japanese for further relocation to ten internment camps in several states. Toyo Miyatake, the man in the beret, kept a photographic diary of life at Manzanar, a camp at the foot of the Sierra. He later returned to Los Angeles and managed a photographic studio in Little Tokyo until his death in 1979.

Elderly Japanese-Americans, veterans of World War II relocation, behind a metal wire fence at Little Tokyo redevelopment project

Peace, prosperity,
and problem solving

With peace came the return of nylons, the emergence of nuclear possibilities, and extraordinary growing pains in Southern California. With peace also came the return of Lieutenant Commander Richard Nixon of Whittier, who decided to run against Congressman Jerry Voorhis. It was the first of a series of campaigns in which Nixon devised a platform out of patriotism while hinting that his opponent was somehow less loyal.

With peace came thousands upon thousands of new residents, a great many of them ex-servicemen who had passed through Los Angeles en route to war and decided that in California the climate was ideal and the future bright. This great influx of Americans from other parts of the country created shortages of almost everything, most acutely housing.

With peace came new institutions called think tanks. Santa Monica's RAND Corporation, an acronym for research and development, was one of the first. Then came Cal Tech's Jet Propulsion Laboratory, Systems Development Corporation, Ramo-Wooldridge, and other problem-solving incubators of computers, transistors, and lunar landing vehicles.

And within a few years after peace came a remarkable realignment with Japan. The hated enemy was recast as a partner for prosperity, a competitor in the technological world of automobiles, optical equipment, and electronic appliances.

(Overleaf) Successful Japanese landings on the California coast; fleets of Toyota trucks at the harbor, waiting for inland delivery

1946

Air problem measured and parking metered

The city was stricken in 1946. First there was a national railroad strike, crippling travel and exacerbating shortages of consumer goods. Later a coal strike resulted in serious loss of energy. Then there was the beginning of a vigorous campaign against smog; investigators from the district attorney's office went around collecting evidence against faulty chimneys, rubbish dumps, oil refineries, and industries. The automobile, so fancied by locals, was not yet identified as a major villain of the pollution drama.

And amid train and traffic tie-ups parking meters were introduced onto the local street scene. "Let's not rent out the streets," raged a *Times* editorial. "Once the parking meters get their foot in the door . . . they will be increasingly hard to oust." Meters have been on the scene, happily and unhappily, ever since; the penny meter has been gradually replaced by meters demanding nickels, dimes, and sometimes quarters. They have moved into residential neighborhoods to help protect homeowner parking and sometimes have been removed from commercial neighborhoods to encourage new business. The ultimate verdict—whether meters generate local revenue or local anguish—remains to be delivered.

Platoons of parking meters stand guard at California State University, Los Angeles

A big brown bag in the sky

Smog, a linguistic blend of smoke and fog, was the new public enemy, a man-made blight so despised that the California legislature passed a law against it in 1947 by a vote of 73 to 1. But smog, a photochemical combination that results in eye-irritating and throat-rasping poisons, could not be banished simply by legislative order. The blue Los Angeles sky, so loved by ailing elders and by aviators, has been screened by browns and grays for decades.

The automobiles that brought the continuing influx of new residents, including a disproportionate number of ex-servicemen, simply added to the problem. In 1947 the first section of the new Hollywood Freeway opened in Cahuenga Pass. In time the equally new Los Angeles Air Pollution Control District would discover that smog was more a by-product of personal mobility than of industrial impurity, further clouding the issue.

Dodger Stadium, with the city in the smoggy background (aerial view from KMPC helicopter)

A community fed through a tube

As early as 1931 electronics pioneer Lee De Forest made the startling prediction for Los Angeles audiences that by 1981 "television sets will be in every modern home." In the same year Don Lee Broadcasting tested a daily television scanning system at radio station KHJ. By 1936 Don Lee was offering "sight-sound" broadcasting. But not until 1948 did television begin to proliferate throughout the city and the entire country.

Between 1948 and 1949 the number of sets in local homes increased more than fourfold, with one small screen in half the households. The motion picture and radio industries were worried about the ensuing competition. Radio would recover thanks to automobile radios and transistor sets. The film industry continued to feel the pinch of competition until eventually television became the primary customer for motion pictures.

Los Angeles prospered as more and more television production moved to the California coast. Whether television is contemporary society's best teacher or its most omnipresent menace remains a national issue. But television continues to be a dominant factor in local life, made here as well as watched here.

(Overleaf) Five-year-olds Jennifer Parham and Katherine Doppelhammer admire a bank of TV images at the Broadway department store in Pasadena

265

1949

Beginning a brand-new beach

Air and space and seclusion were once the virtues of Southern California beaches. Conveniently removed from the periodic building frenzy downtown, they were several sand castles away from movie studios hammering around Hollywood.

But the postwar years witnessed increased numbers of residents, especially World War II veterans, moving into the areas along the strand. Aircraft industries had grown up alongside the ocean, and as communities from Redondo to Santa Monica to Malibu were expanding, a carnival of hedonistic activities was being introduced. Weight lifters forced their way into the Santa Monica neighborhood. Boxing bouts were staged for weekend amusement. Beauty contests, formerly concentrated at Venice, were being judged all along the coast. In 1949 the beaches became a strip of leisure for laid-off workers, where they could play volleyball, swap flight stories, and ease the pains of a minor recession.

The shadow of the aerospace industry permanently transformed the beaches from infrequent weekend retreats to everyday playgrounds. Only at Playa del Rey, where the air traffic roars directly overhead and a residential neighborhood has been razed to clear the flight path, is there a semblance of the splendid sandy isolation that used to mark the littoral.

A jumbo jet shadowed on the beach at Playa del Rey

1950

The power to a tract

Sprawl was still an acceptable word in 1950. The single-family detached residence, attractive or not, continued to be the ideal. Large tracts of land were bought, subdivided, and covered with look-alike dwellings. The freeways would make the scheme work; the blight of smog was still thought to be produced by industry, not by the automobile.

Lakewood, Louis Boyar's development south of the city, was a perfect example of the mass-produced environment. Boyar bought up 3,375 acres of former farmland. He projected a population of 70,000, with 17,000 homes along with self-contained shopping areas—a community twice the size of Levittown in New York. Within two years, more than half of Lakewood was built, a complete town without the responsibilities of its own municipal police, fire, and health-care protection. Lakewood purchased its necessary services from Los Angeles County, thus establishing a contractual pattern later applied to dozens of unincorporated communities in the region.

Many of the 1950 values persist, although most people by now have learned the lessons of smog and the perils of plowing under farmland for single-family frame residences.

Houses being hammered up in Rowland Heights

1951

A break in the basin

The unquenchable local thirst prompted the construction of Baldwin Hills Reservoir, a large man-made lake atop a hillside in a residential neighborhood. Dedication ceremonies took place in April 1951, while California was still arguing with Arizona over the amount of water that could be imported from the Colorado River.

The Baldwin Hills basin burst in 1963. A mighty wall of water gushed through a seventy-five-foot split in the dam. Within the next eighty minutes five people were drowned and $13 million worth of property was washed down the hill. There were 65 houses totally destroyed and more than 210 other residences seriously damaged.

The earth had moved. No one quite knew why. The hole in the hilltop has never been fixed. Los Angeles County now owns 200 acres of land in the vicinity, including the reservoir and surrounding acreage, and plans to build a park where the water basin used to be.

Baldwin Hills Reservoir from the air—a rupture unrepaired

1952

Racism in residence

Shortage of private housing in Los Angeles was still a major political and economic problem in 1952. Mayor Fletcher Bowron proposed building government-subsidized units for poor people. His critics denounced the plan as "socialized" housing and threatened a recall campaign.

At the time black citizens were moving west within the city, and some families settled into the West Adams district, a neighborhood of large estates above Exposition Park. Resentment was soon expressed with bombs exploding at black-owned homes. Damage to buildings was considerable, but the harm to civic peace was worse. Racial prejudice was translated into acts of criminal violence: white bigots were using force to keep blacks in their place. The bombings brought about their own backlash; reasonable citizens of both races condemned the violation of human rights, and the westward movement among Los Angeles's blacks continued.

The ghetto around Watts remained the primary area where newly arrived blacks could find a home in Los Angeles. In the late 1970s, in an attempt to upgrade residential opportunity, the local government would move middle-class housing to Watts, eastward from the Playa del Rey area near the airport. Homes that had been in the flight path of big jets were doomed by noise. The city had them transported across town and sold at public auction, but by that time nobody called it socialism.

Citizens in Watts at a city-sponsored housing auction

1953

A new balance of power

The year 1953 began by ending a recurrent humiliation. Since 1947, when the football powers of the Pacific Coast started bringing Big Ten teams to the Rose Bowl, Midwest teams had been the winners. Illinois beat UCLA. Michigan trampled USC. Northwestern triumphed over UC Berkeley. So did Ohio State. Then it was Michigan's turn again in 1951. In 1952 Illinois came back to savage Stanford.

According to the prophets of sport, California simply could not compete. The Big Ten was much too tough. Cold winters apparently produced stronger linemen. Californians played football; midwesterners worked at it.

The myth finally was destroyed in 1953, when USC beat Wisconsin 7 to 0. Jubilant fans danced in the streets of Pasadena. The grand marshall for the parade that year was the young vice-president from California, Richard M. Nixon, a man who often made political points with sports metaphors.

By the 1970s the former Big Ten domination was merely a memory. California teams were winning more than their share of Rose Bowl games, and USC was the dominant school—in football.

The football Trojans of USC

A ban against burning

Smog persisted as the major irritant of local life. Reporters continued to record the search for scientific answers to air pollution. Scientists analyzed a variety of smog-producing problems, including industry, public utilities, and automobiles. When the backyard incinerator, where the householder burned trash, was cited as one of the major sources of smog, the county Board of Supervisors in October 1954 banned trash incineration, a law still in force. Yet smog levels were not noticeably lowered by the prohibition.

These days backyard burning often occurs by tragic accident, which happened in 1978 when another fire swept from San Fernando Valley over the Santa Monica Mountains and onto the affluent sands of Malibu, destroying valuable tracts of land and hundreds of homes along the way.

Among the ashes of the 1978 Malibu fire

A magic kingdom among amusement parks

Walt Disney did it, built the nation's number one tourist attraction on nearly seventy-three acres of former orange groves in Anaheim. Creating Fantasyland in a region already famous for fantasy, Disney scaled his own Matterhorn, cultivated his own jungle, sponsored the first California monorail, hammered up a small-town Main Street—and kept it all remarkably clean.

Millions of Americans have trudged to Southern California to sample the charms of Disneyland. Because of Disneyland, Anaheim has become a major convention city and dozens of hotels do capacity business all year round. The California Angels baseball team moved to Anaheim partly because the national pastime wanted to be near the national amusement park. The Los Angeles Rams football team moved to Anaheim too, partly because Walt Disney had transformed an agricultural Anaheim into a year-round attraction.

Orange County was considered part of Los Angeles when the original Mexican settlers trekked to the pueblo. It is now the county that Los Angeles citizens head for to escape the big city, either for a day in Tomorrowland or for retirement in suburban land.

Disneyland electrical parade

1956

The sky's new limit

By 1956 downtown real estate interests were eyeing airspace for expanded office construction. Los Angeles had originally set a ceiling on building heights because of the frequency of earthquakes in the vicinity; 140 feet was as high as structures could be built. Only City Hall had been allowed to scrape the sky above thirteen stories.

But new materials and structural techniques promised quake resistance. Engineers, developers, architects, and speculators viewed high-rise density as the only way Los Angeles could grow, and now, in 1956, the building codes were changed. Down came the limits. Up went the towers.

In the early 1970s the silhouette of Los Angeles leaped skyward. Security Pacific Plaza, designed by Albert C. Martin & Associates, rises fifty-five stories above Bunker Hill. It is faced with granite and flanked by a park with a waterfall. United California Bank, on lower ground downtown, reaches to sixty-two stories. Bank of America Tower, part of Atlantic Richfield Plaza, takes high finance to fifty-two stories.

Security Pacific Bank headquarters on Bunker Hill; sculpture by Alexander Calder

1957

Homage to the arts

The new building for the Otis Art Institute, named after its original benefactor, publisher Harrison Gray Otis, was opened in 1957. In 1885 Otis had bought one of the first lots within Gaylord Wilshire's Parkview and built a home facing Westlake Park. In 1917 he donated the ground to Los Angeles County for an arts school, which was opened in 1918.

By 1978 government bureaucracy and budget austerity forced the Otis faculty and students to search for a new sponsor, the Parsons School of Design in New York, where the emphasis is on professional training. The county Board of Supervisors approved the Parsons merger; the grand design now spans a continent.

Sculpture class at Otis Art Institute, now a West Coast branch of Parsons School of Design

1958

A farewell to old Bunker Hill

By 1958 the first of the new tall buildings, California Bank, was rising downtown to top out at eighteen stories. The Dodgers had moved west, and everybody was talking about Los Angeles's making the big leagues in 1958. And the federal government approved Bunker Hill as a downtown redevelopment area.

Bunker Hill had begun life as Prudent Beaudry's subdivision in 1874. Bunker Hill was fashionable from the beginning—grand Gothic and Victorian houses predominated—but by the 1950s, with the freeways carrying commuters into the suburbs, the residential section of downtown was sadly run-down.

Preservationists insisted on saving some of the architectural relics, hoping to relocate rather than remove them. A plan was developed to create Heritage Square, a museum of nineteenth-century houses settled on a stretch of land in Highland Park directly north of downtown. A couple of the moves from Bunker Hill were failures; two houses burned down before relocation could begin. But Hale House, built in Highland Park during the 1880s, is a restored example of what Queen Anne–Eastlake housing was like on Bunker Hill. Even the original color combination has been repainted on its ornate face.

Hale House, a cornerstone of Heritage Square alongside the Pasadena Freeway at Highland Park

1959

Another saving grace, in Watts

Local bureaucrats decided to pull the towers down in 1959, citing them as a public nuisance instead of recognizing them as an extraordinary example of folk art and fantastic architecture. Simon Rodia, by himself, had built his towers over a period of thirty-three years. He had no drawn plans, no machines, no scaffolding, no welding equipment. What he had was an aesthetic dream: "I had in mind to do something big, and I did."

He built big and tall with found materials—scrap tiles, discarded bottles, abandoned bed frames, seashells, and old pieces of pipe. The material was junk. The result was three towers—one ninety-nine feet tall, another ninety-seven feet, and the third fifty-five feet—

that have become internationally famous. Rodia walked away from them in 1954, to move to Martinez, California.

The city wanted to take the towers down because no building permit had been issued. A citizens' committee came to the rescue in 1959. Members raised money as well as artistic consciousness and proved by engineering tests that the towers had extraordinary structural stability. The remarkable work was saved, although vandals and weather have damaged the towers in recent years. The city, which now owns and appreciates the property, performs restoration duties and exercises preservation responsibility.

Simon Rodia's towers near the railroad tracks at Watts

1960

Sporting life goes public

A new decade opened with grandstand plays by Los Angeles. The Democratic National Convention took over the town in 1960, the first national convention ever held in Los Angeles. At the brand-new Sports Arena in Exposition Park, John F. Kennedy was picked as the presidential candidate and went on to beat California's native son, Richard Nixon, in the election.

The Dodgers' grandstand, a stadium in Chavez Ravine, was constructed, upsetting a group of organized citizens who demanded a park rather than a ballpark in their area.

And the swimming pool had become a symbol of the pleasure-seeking way

of life in Los Angeles. More than 20 percent of all the pools in the United States were Southern California water holes. Lawns were suddenly bedecked with squares or kidneys or rectangles of water; a pool meant many things to many people—status, landscaping, property value—and it continued as a favorite fenced-in show of affluence until the tennis craze rallied in the 1970s and the drop shot displaced the swan dive.

(Overleaf) Private tennis courts and swimming pools set the pattern for life-style and landscape in Los Angeles

287

1961

A campaign for rubbish reform
Sam Yorty was a self-made maverick, exactly the kind of man to govern a city that was never quite sure what to save, what to change. Yorty came from the Midwest, a liberal politician with populist views. Then he changed sides to become a red-baiting congressman with conservative views. By 1961 he was campaigning for mayor of Los Angeles, and he chose, as his gut issue, garbage.

Following the ban on backyard incinerators in the early 1950s, Los Angeles residents had to separate their trash—wet garbage segregated from dry—for municipal pickup. The procedure was not only inconvenient and time-consuming, but smelly as well. Yorty ran on a rubbish integration ticket, promising householders he would reunite trash for collection. He won, beating incumbent Norris Poulson by a whisker—or four table scraps.

Yorty went on to win three terms as mayor, to bolt the Democratic party for the Republican party, and to make unsuccessful runs for the Senate and the governorship. He became a staunch Nixon supporter even after Watergate, and he hosted his own television talk show where his maverick voice made him a media celebrity.

Sam Yorty, at home in San Fernando Valley, dropping trash into his trash container

1962

A city within a city within an old movie lot

The concept of Century City seemed to combine right place with right time. In the early 1960s urban renewal and redevelopment were becoming the new national pastimes: take a piece of city and, with public or private funds, remodel it into a spanking new environment.

The movie studios had shrunk by the 1960s; giant sound stages were less appealing than real locations, and independent filmmakers used the entire world for their back lots. Alcoa invested in most of the area that was formerly taken up by Twentieth Century-Fox, a large hunk of land between Beverly Hills and Westwood Village. Fox retained a small corner for homegrown illusions, while Alcoa began building a promised "city within a city," a development with an ideal mix of office buildings, residences, and shopping facilities. Some of the country's most distinguished architects—I. M. Pei, Minoru Yamasaki, Gyo Obata—plus some of the most important local firms—Becket, Luckman, Martin, Starkman—would design and build the structures.

The gateway buildings by Becket were under way by 1962. The Yamasaki towers were built by 1975. During the intervening years Century City developed as a center for offices, a commercial competitor for retail sales with Beverly Hills, a high- and medium-rise architectural showcase. But only the rich could afford to live and work there; other daytime occupants had to commute. The Pei-designed apartments are a long walk from the shopping center and there is insufficient separation between auto and pedestrian traffic, but the subcity is an otherwise successful blend of modern commercial and residential complexes.

Century Plaza Towers, twin triangles designed by Minoru Yamasaki as the centerpieces for Century City

1963

A bridge between ports, between people

A city in which most of the rivers are narrow and seasonally run dry needs few monumental bridges. Los Angeles had none until 1963, when the one-mile Vincent Thomas Bridge—named after the assemblyman for the area at that time—was opened between San Pedro and Terminal Island. The suspension bridge, a span hanging 185 feet above the water, would link industry on the island with commerce on the mainland.

What might be called a sociological bridge was built the same year downtown. Tom Bradley, Gilbert Lindsay, and Billy Mills were elected to the fifteen-member City Council, the first blacks to be chosen as Los Angeles legislators. Equal opportunity—in both employment and schools—was an acute local political issue; with the 1963 election more than lip service would at last be paid to this problem. Although progress was being extolled in the political arena at the time, no Hispanics had yet joined council with Anglo and black elected leaders.

Vincent Thomas Bridge, from San Pedro to Terminal Island

1964

Culture comes home

By 1964 Los Angeles was still more rough diamond than cultured pearl. Theaters and concert halls were often halfhearted afterthoughts; the Philharmonic had to perform in a church-owned hall downtown, and many of the best plays in town were created on campus at UCLA. There was an urgent need in such a large city for an arts center.

Civic leader Dorothy Chandler convinced the politicians, launched the campaign, and directed the designers to build a home for the performing arts —music, theater, and dance—on the hill above the Civic Center downtown. In December 1964 the Dorothy Chandler Pavilion, first of three theaters in the Music Center complex, was inaugurated. The acoustics were excellent. Municipal pride was even louder; at last culture had its proper setting, a physical presence as impressive as the performers who live and play in Los Angeles.

Dorothy Chandler onstage at the Music Center Pavilion

1965

And a new setting for the visual arts

The new county art museum at Hancock Park opened one year after the inauguration of the Music Center. Exhibitions of the visual arts had previously shared space with natural history in Exposition Park, an unlikely if not uncomfortable relationship. But by the early 1960s the painting and sculpture communities of Los Angeles were enjoying extraordinary attention—along gallery row on La Cienega, in studios at Venice, among select dealers in Beverly Hills.

Art collector Edward Carter, a retailing executive, led the museum campaign much the way Dorothy Chandler had waged the performing arts battle: by persuading civic leaders and business tycoons that Los Angeles should value serious culture as much as it honored hilarity.

The museum, designed by William Pereira & Associates, was built on old tar-pit territory at Hancock Park and opened in 1965 with bands playing in its plaza.

(Overleaf) Giant Pool Balls Plexiglass *by Claes Oldenburg, foreground, and* Parallel Piped Vents *by Ron Davis, on the wall, in the contemporary gallery of the Los Angeles County Museum of Art*

295

1966

Hair and hipness and Hare Krishna

The late 1960s were to become a disturbing period in American society, especially in conflict with the established values. Strange times started on Sunset Boulevard; streams of exotically costumed young people, tuned to a new kind of pulsating music, were clogging the streets. Strange hours began in the classrooms, heated arguments about how long a young man might wear his hair. The Beatles had brought social change off the tops of their heads. Rock music became the poetry of youthful alienation, drugs reflected a new morality, which many elders viewed as a dangerous model for their children.

The youth movement seemed to have erupted almost overnight—hippies taking over from the beat generation, flower children protesting the war in Vietnam and urging peace in ways sometimes aggressive, a mandate issuing from the young "not to trust anyone over thirty." Students battled police, on campus, on the avenue, on the beach. Dropping out—of school, of the establishment, of the consensus —became a positive negative stand.

Many of the young people returned to the fold and looked, behaved, and adjusted just as their parents had. Many other young people stayed out through the 1970s, discovered other

ways to live—at rural communes or within Eastern-based religions. The Hare Krishnas, with ritualistic roots in India, became one of the most visible groups of young people promoting a new way of life in the 1960s that would continue through the 1970s.

Hare Krishna annual Festival of the Chariots; raising consciousness and costumes at Venice Beach

1967

Bulldozers begin lowering Bunker Hill

The razing of the houses on Bunker Hill was completed by 1967. The grading of 136 downtown acres—a federally funded urban-renewal project—was under way. But, as renewal proceeded, this residential neighborhood nearest downtown would become the next focus for business downtown. The financial spine of the city was shifting west from Spring Street to Flower and Figueroa near the Harbor Freeway. When the downtown project was eventually completed, the new Union Bank headquarters would put its vault within Bunker Hill. Arco Plaza would build just beyond Bunker boundaries.

The shiny Bonaventure Hotel would mirror the nearby renewal. Security Pacific would climb the hill.

The apartment units known as Bunker Hill Towers reclaimed some of the lost residential space, but only for the well-to-do. Urban renewal for the next decade would translate into commerce, not housing. Not until the late 1970s would the city and its Community Redevelopment Agency make commitments to bring round-the-clock residential life back to downtown.

Earth-moving west of Hill Street, for senior-citizen housing at Bunker Hill

1968

A coroner presides over controversy

Robert Kennedy was struck down when he was about to enjoy a California triumph of his own. He had just won the presidential primary, a milestone on the way to the 1968 national convention. As he was leaving the ballroom at the Ambassador Hotel by a back door through the pantry and kitchen, surrounded by family and friends, he was assassinated.

Martin Luther King had been assassinated in Memphis only two months earlier. President John Kennedy had been assassinated in Dallas nearly five years earlier. Now the horror had shifted to Los Angeles.

Thomas Noguchi performed the autopsy on Robert Kennedy and provided the medical evidence that would be argued—like the evidence in the JFK and Martin Luther King killings—for the next decade. Noguchi had already weathered attacks—some called them political, others called them racist—within county government. Now he would justify his department's findings in the death of a national leader.

Three years later the same coroner prepared the forensic medical evidence following the sensational Manson family killings, Los Angeles's most tragic case of mass murder and mutilation. Amid some of the ugliest crimes and most vociferous political arguments of the decade, Noguchi persisted, an authority in his field.

(Overleaf) Thomas Noguchi, chief medical examiner for Los Angeles County, an authority on assassination and mass murder

299

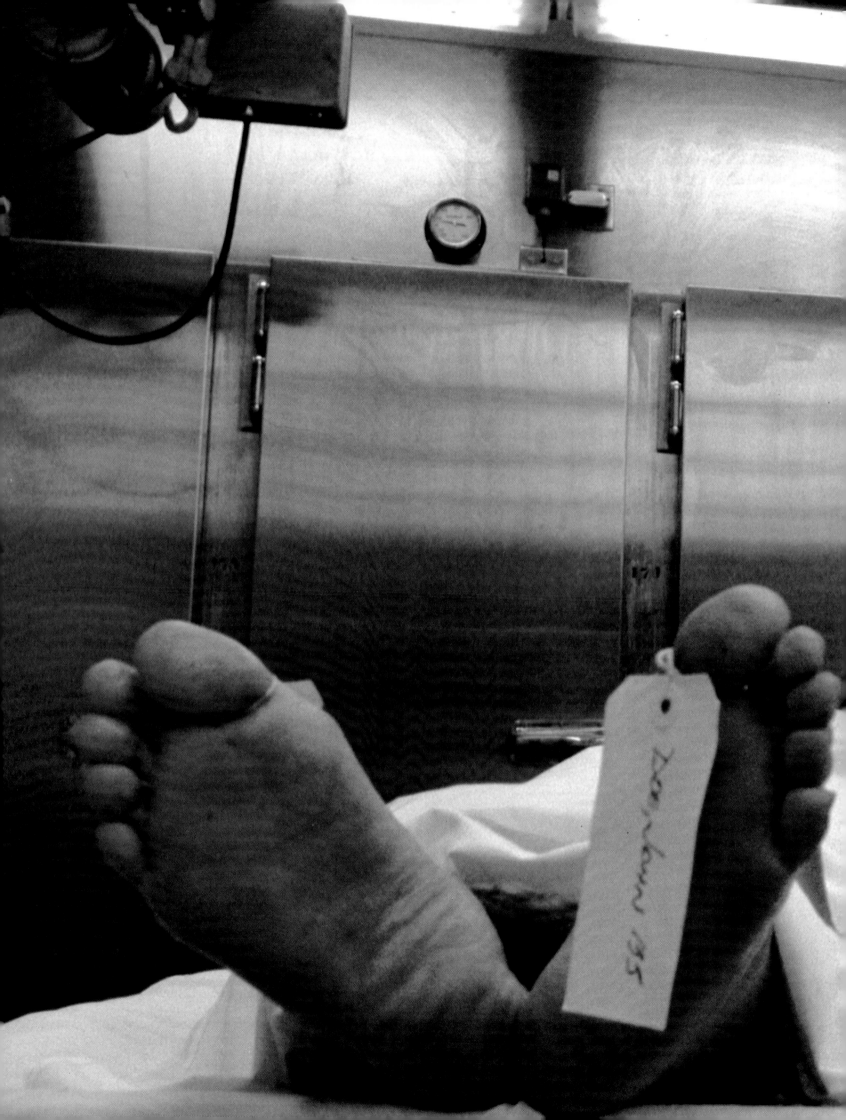

*A municipal–county marriage
on the sands*

Los Angeles City and Los Angeles
County merged beach interests and responsibilities in 1969, a marriage that
has proved tranquil, at least at the
waterline. But in many other areas the
city and the county do not always
live together happily ever after. Not
when a city of three million people is
surrounded by a county more than
twice as populous. Not when the county has one law enforcement group—the
sheriff's department—and the city has
its own police force. Not when each
government has its own fire fighters,
separate library and school systems,
and other overlapping services or juris-
dictions.

The citizens of Los Angeles City
figure they pay a disproportionate
amount of property taxes to sustain
such duplication, which to them
amounts to waste. Outlying Los Angeles County citizens complain the city
dominates their lives; they are convinced their government is too remote
and unresponsive to deliver adequate
services. Moves to consolidate those
services continue to rouse local controversy, including suggestions to amal-
gamate the governments into one com-
prehensive metropolitan body.

*Surfers walk their boards by sun-
set at Malibu*

1970

Decision to desegregate

In 1970 Judge Alfred Gitelson, a reasonably conservative and relatively reflective Republican, ordered desegregation of the Los Angeles schools. He was merely following Supreme Court precedents and responding to evidence that in Los Angeles separate was not equal. He was simply demanding that the children of blacks and Hispanics—more than half the school population—be integrated into the public school system. Five years after the burning of Watts, Gitelson was ordering an end to ghetto education.

His life was threatened for his troubles. His campaign for reelection was undone at the polls, a rare case of a superior court judge being unseated. A new decade of controversy over school integration had begun. Many pro-integration residents admitted that busing was the only practical means of fairly mixing races in a sprawling city. Anti-integrationists, on the other hand, insisted that busing was cruel and unusual treatment, foreshadowing the death of the neighborhood school.

Although Gitelson had never specifically advised busing as the means to integration, it quickly became the scapegoat. Still under attack, the bus these days has a dwindling number of white students to transport, a relatively constant number of blacks, and an increasing number of Hispanics.

Anglo children are now a minority in the system, as a result of white flight and birth control. The arguments continue; the buses roll; and the school system is still not integrated.

A busload of black children en route to school—crosstown

1971

A decade begins with earthquakes and near depression

Politicians and ordinary citizens alike were comparing the slump of 1971 to the Great Depression of the 1930s. The county Board of Supervisors was so anxious about the economy that its members ordered a freeze on hiring, postponed approval on purchasing, declared a moratorium on public building, and fretted about how to meet a $23 million welfare bill by June. Suddenly the affluent county of Los Angeles seemed nearly $60 million in the red. In addition, there was an earthquake.

The city of Los Angeles was facing a $7.5 million deficit as the cost of local government inflated nearly 13 percent annually and revenues increased at less than 6 percent. Bankers wanted to be optimistic, reminding the citizens that of the six largest cities in the United States only Los Angeles had managed to stay in the black during the 1930s.

But the twin demons of unemployment and inflation were hurting the work force and the elected officials simultaneously. The California ethic under Governor Ronald Reagan became cut, squeeze, trim—at least until the next year.

Out of work, luck, and money— downtown

1972

The shopping center moves back to downtown

For years the suburban shopping center had brought retail trade out of the central city to meet the sprawl at its edges. The suburban center had contributed to the economic deterioration of downtown, where the stores were older and parking was inconvenient. Broadway Plaza, like Arco Plaza, was a 1970s attempt to lure commerce back to the center of town where office commuters come to work. Broadway Plaza, a 1972–73 project by Charles Luckman, introduced a Hyatt Regency Hotel into the mix of offices and shops; visitors could browse alongside occupants of the thirty-two-story tower.

Some critics complained bitterly about a whole square block of brick that seemed to turn its back to the rest of the city along Seventh Street. Others responded positively to the two-level mall enclosed by the Broadway store, the hotel, and the offices—a plaza walled in wood and brick under a skylight framed in steel. The light from above was a little like the surprise of the interior stairwell of the nineteenth-century Bradbury Building. The form was reminiscent of some of the great railroad terminals.

Broadway Plaza, a combination of department store, offices, hotel, retail shops, and skylit atrium

1973

Oil embargo, a cruel joke on the city of automobiles

The energy crisis in the fall of 1973 caught most Americans completely off guard, causing the miseries the nation has had to adjust to ever since: lines at gasoline stations, shortages of fuel oil, ever-skyrocketing prices for the mobility that Southern Californians took for granted for so long.

The Arab world was meting out punishments—cutback in production, a rise in oil prices, and a boycott by some Mideast nations of sales to the United States—because of American support for Israel in the 1973 resumption of warfare.

Oil itself had become a weapon. Dependence on Arab oil reflected the general American automotive way of life; domestic crude to fuel the nation's engines was not plentiful enough. Los Angeles, the city framed by freeway systems, was particularly stricken. Without mass transit, beyond a marginal bus system, the city was on the verge of becoming an obsolete center of commerce, culture, and manufacturing.

There were fistfights and even shootings at the gasoline pumps. The national speed limit was set at 55 miles an hour. Conservation, at least for a time, became an active policy, not only a slogan. But gradually, over the next six years, people drifted back to their old driving habits, simply paying more for the privilege. When there was another crisis, in 1979, and the gas lines formed again, Los Angeles residents at last realized that shortage was something they would have to learn to live with and gas guzzling something they would have to do without.

(Overleaf) The annual Halloween pumpkin painting on Union Oil's 80,000-barrel gasoline tank at Wilmington

Gift from a modern Medici

In 1974 oil tycoon J. Paul Getty presented Los Angeles with a wondrous replica of a first-century Roman villa. The original Villa dei Papyri was buried when Mount Vesuvius erupted in A.D. 79 and remained so until major excavation work during the eighteenth century unearthed it. The Getty villa, situated directly above post-and-beam residences in Pacific Palisades, houses a museum of Greek and Roman antiquities, with extraordinary works from the fourth century through the Renaissance and into the twentieth century.

Architectural historians David Gebhard and Robert Winter have compared the Getty Museum to "Southern California as it should be—the past as seen through the perceptive eyes of the 1970s, and a landscape which puts the old world of the Mediterranean to shame." But the nice ironies cannot be ignored: a Roman-style palace perched above unstable land; a great public gift, from a man who made his multimillions in the oil industry, opened one year after the first oil crunch overwhelmed California; a place for public enjoyment requiring advance reservations because of a shortage of public parking. Nevertheless, Getty's museum is a major tribute to the new aesthetic awakening in Southern California.

J. Paul Getty Museum at Pacific Palisades

A new history on another hill

On the opposite side of town from the Getty, in the hills above the Pasadena Rose Bowl, a strong, dark, sleek new building was taking shape in 1975 on behalf of the arts. It was made of steel and glass, a structure 672 feet long, black on the outside and black and white inside. While the Getty design pays homage to the graces of antiquity, the Art Center College of Design honors a modern mandate for beauty in severity. The building was designed by Craig Ellwood, a builder turned designer and, after completion of the school, turned painter. He had always wanted to put one of his elegant boxes astride a canyon.

Pasadenans were puzzled by the $8.6 million worth of austerity being built. Student bodies were arguing over whether it was an attractive environment for study and work or a cold statement of rigidity. But by 1976 Mayor Tim Matthews labeled it magnificent, and Bill Lacy, then head of the National Endowment for the Arts architectural program, referred to it as "a moving emotional experience." In either case, Art Center changed the face of the hills, and one of the nation's leading campuses of industrial design brought an extraordinary modern package to Pasadena.

Art Center College of Design, a bridge of a building across the San Rafael Hills in Pasadena

1976

The freeways paved with diamonds
Nothing infuriated locals as much as the gas crunch until the Diamond Lanes were introduced in 1976. They were designed to encourage car pooling, stimulate expanded bus use, and thereby conserve energy. Caltrans, the state transportation department, decided that during rush hours the inner—fast—lane of the Santa Monica Freeway would be reserved for car pools and buses. The inner lane in each direction was painted with diamonds, the new symbol of preferential treatment.

The results were confusing, although dramatic: while traffic dropped about 3 percent across the Santa Monica and bus usage increased from 1,000 to 4,000 passengers a day from the west side, accidents rose with tempers. Impatient, frustrated, hotheaded motorists took to dangerous shiftings and jockeyings on and off the freeway ramps, in and out of the Diamond Lanes. A public interest suit, claiming that the state agency had not complied with federal and state environmental laws prior to applying the diamonds, was filed against Caltrans. The suit was successful.

After what urban affairs writer Ray Hebert called "nearly five months of turmoil, confusion, and adverse reactions," the Diamond Lanes were pronounced dead by a court order.

Auto graveyard at Carson near the San Diego Freeway

1977

And a Beverly Hills street paved with gold
Rodeo Drive's shopping area is only two and a half blocks long, but by 1977 its rents were sky-high. In the early 1970s a merchant might have been able to rent retail space along that small strip for as little as one dollar a square foot. By 1975, with Gucci's monogram on display and other international fashion plates arriving on the scene, rents were doubled and firms were being charged "key fees" of $35,000 for the right to open their doors. By the end of 1977 rents doubled again and $150,000 was the fee paid by a potential tenant for the right to take over a lease.

Public relations people called Rodeo the gold-paved drive. Gucci's rent alone was $16,000 a month. Hermes, Sassoon, Giorgio, Courreges, Van Cleef & Arpels, Elizabeth Arden, Theodore, Lapidus, Carroll, Jon Peters, and other well-dropped names were fancy neighbors. Europeans flew in to buy American luxuries since the relative value of the dollar was declining. Asians came to invest in real estate. Arabs translated oil riches into material splendor.

Beverly Hills was squarely the focus of the new boom, selling $412 million worth of retail goods in 1977, $100 million along little Rodeo. Property values on the drive had increased 300 percent during the three preceding years. And the Rodeo rush—goods as gold—continues as the entire world comes to Southern California for a whole world of things.

Window of Gucci on Rodeo Drive in Beverly Hills

1978

Another natural disaster

The Malibu fire of 1978 began at Agoura, in San Fernando Valley, another assault against a region famous for big burns followed by flooding, for earth tremors and droughts and landslides. It was set by an arsonist while the Santa Ana winds were gusting hot, dry air off the desert toward the coast.

The fire leaped across the Santa Monica Mountains, searing 25,000 acres of brush and destroying 161 homes before sizzling out at sea. Some 300 animals were killed at a breeding ranch along the way; more than fifty people were injured, either trapped by the fire or fighting it; more than fifty homes were seriously damaged, in addition to those completely destroyed. During the same week there were three other major fires—in Mandeville Canyon, in Carbon Canyon across the Orange County border, and in the mountains above Sierra Madre.

Los Angeles learns slowly, but after the 1978 fires the use of wooden shingles on hillside roofs was strictly prohibited.

The charred remains of hillside residences along Malibu Beach

1979

Snow drops across the desert

Since sunshine is the only anticipated weather in Southern California, people were totally unprepared when snow fell in early 1979. In Palm Springs a major golf tournament had to be canceled. In Antelope Valley fourteen inches of snow fell, which forced the closing of Interstate 5, the main north–south artery in California. And in Castaic, at the northern end of San Fernando Valley, one hundred motorists had to abandon their cars and seek emergency overnight accommodations at the local school.

Wherever snow did not blanket the ground, rain drenched it. There was a rain-induced power failure in Paramount, a mammoth mudslide onto the Pacific Coast Highway at Malibu, and a sunken fishing boat at San Pedro.

Los Angeles—the city normally blessed by warmth and interminably bathed by sun—habitually refuses to acknowledge any exceptions to the temperate rule. And yet exceptions keep occurring, as regularly as almost every year for the past 200 wet-dry, fire-flooded, shaken-landslid years.

White-capped Joshua trees in Antelope Valley

1980

The pleasure persists, along with the people

After 200 years, Los Angeles is the most fascinating piece of unfinished urban business left in the United States. Perhaps it is still too soon to tell what Los Angeles will be like when it grows up. But the next years are bound to offer historic answers to contemporary questions.

What will this city be like as Hispanics again become the largest population group in a once-Mexican settlement?

How will Los Angeles adjust to huge new communities of Asians—including refugees from China, Cambodia, Vietnam, Korea, Thailand, and other Eastern nations?

Will the automobile ever be surpassed as the principal vehicle for trade and travel?

When and where will the next major earthquake shake?

Has the community learned how to conserve against the next major drought?

Can engineers find a means of pro-

tecting the city against the next major slide?

Is smog conquerable?

Is this crazy quilt of a human settlement stitched together for good as well as forever?

Maybe nobody knows. But that's why we persist in living along this irregular coast—because we like it, because we choose to live where the end of every story is unpredictable.